Also by Stephen W. Garber, Ph.D., Marianne Daniels Garber, Ph.D., and Robyn Freedman Spizman:

GOOD BEHAVIOR: OVER 1,200 SOLUTIONS TO YOUR CHILD'S PROBLEMS FROM BIRTH TO AGE TWELVE

If Your
Child Is
Hyperactive,
Inattentive,
Impulsive,
Distractible . . .

Helping
the
ADD (Attention
. . . Deficit
Disorder)
Hyperactive
Child

If Your Child Is Hyperactive, Inattentive, Impulsive, Distractible . . .

Stephen W. Garber, Ph.D.

Marianne Daniels Garber, Ph.D.

Robyn Freedman Spizman

Helping
the
ADD (Attention
Deficit
Disorder)
Hyperactive
Child

VILLARD BOOKS · NEW YORK · 1993

Library of Congress Cataloging-in-Publication
Data
Garber, Stephen W.
   If your child is hyperactive, inattentive,
impulsive, distractible . . . /Stephen W.
Garber, Marianne Daniels Garber, and Robyn
Freedman Spizman.
      p. cm.
   ISBN 0-394-57205-X
   1. Attention deficit disorders.
2. Hyperactive child syndrome.
I. Garber, Marianne Daniels.   II. Spizman,
Robyn Freedman.   III. Title.
RJ496.A86G35   1990
649'.153—dc20   90-35992

9   8   7

DESIGNED BY BARBARA MARKS

With special thanks and appreciation this book is dedicated to the parents, children and teachers from whom we have learned so much as we work together to solve the problems associated with attention deficit disorder and hyperactivity; and to our families, friends and colleagues who support us through all our endeavors.

■ Contents

List of Figures *xi*
Preface *xv*

1. **MY CHILD HAS WHAT?** *3*

2. **HOW TO TELL IF YOUR CHILD REALLY HAS ADHD** *17*

3. **MOTIVATING YOUR CHILD** *35*

4. **HOW TO EXPLAIN ADHD TO YOUR CHILD** *52*

5. **GAINING ACCEPTANCE AND SUPPORT FROM SIBLINGS, OTHER RELATIVES, FRIENDS, TEACHERS AND OTHERS** *64*

6. **IF, WHEN AND HOW TO USE MEDICATION** *72*

7. **CONTROLLING ACTIVITY LEVEL** *89*

8. **CALMNESS TRAINING** *108*

9. **IMPULSE CONTROL TRAINING** *117*

10. **BEATING DISTRACTIONS** *127*

11. **STRETCHING ATTENTION SPAN** *140*

12. **FOLLOWING RULES** *152*

13. **CONTROLLING AGGRESSION** *164*

14. **BUILDING SELF-ESTEEM** *174*

15. **THE ADHD CHILD AT PLAY** *184*

16. **THE ADHD CHILD AT SCHOOL** *198*

17. **THE ADHD CHILD GROWN UP** *216*

Appendix A   222
Appendix B   223
Suggested Readings   225
References   228
Index   231

▪ List of Figures

Figure 1.1   The Normal Curve   *15*

Figure 3.1   Record of Verbal Statements   *38*

Figure 3.2   The First National Bank of Points   *42*

Figure 3.3   Jim's Bank of Points   *43*

Figure 3.4   Jim's Bar Graph   *45*

Figure 3.5   A Reinforcer Survey   *47*

Figure 4.1   The Brain as Control Center   *60*

Figure 6.1   Daily Report Card   *85*

Figure 6.2   My Summary Report   *87*

Figure 7.1   Ronnie's Staircase to Success Chart   *92*

Figure 7.2   Statue Staircase to Success Chart   *94*

Figure 7.3   My Point Bank   *95*

Figure 7.4   Clockcard   *100*

Figure 7.5   Walt's Clockcard   *103*

Figure 7.6   Clockcard with Endurance Goals   *106*

Figure 8.1   Relaxation Scoreboard   *114*

Figure 8.2   Relaxation Contract   *116*

Figure 9.1   Impulsive versus Planned Acts   *119*

Figure 9.2   Impulsive Acts and Consequences   *120*

Figure 9.3   "I Am Impulsive" List   *121*

Figure 9.4   "I'm in Control" Card   *122*

Figure 9.5   Carl's "I'm in Control" Card   *123*

Figure 9.6   "I Can Control Myself" List   *125*

Figure 10.1   Greg's List of Distractions   *130*

Figure 10.2   Distract-o-Meters   *131*

Figure 10.3   Zapper Log   *136*

Figure 10.4   Chris's Personal Record   *138*

Figure 11.1   Hints for Paying Attention   *143*

Figure 11.2   Attention Span Tape   *145*
Figure 11.3   "I Can Pay Attention" Card   *146*
Figure 11.4   Jan's Attention Span Tape   *147*
Figure 11.5   Summary Chart   *149*
Figure 12.1   Rule Success   *160*
Figure 12.2   Rule Card   *162*
Figure 12.3   "Rules I Have Mastered" Chart   *163*
Figure 14.1   Negative Self Tapes   *181*
Figure 16.1   Jess's Daily Schedule   *203*
Figure 16.2   Neal's In Seat Record   *209*
Figure 16.3   Report Card   *212*

Throughout the pages of this book, we have used male pronouns when discussing the problems of ADHD children. This is not an oversight on our part, nor does it reflect latent male chauvinism. Rather, our choice reflects the fact that while girls can have many of the characteristics discussed, approximately nine times as many boys as girls are diagnosed as having an attention deficit hyperactivity disorder.

▪ *Preface*

During the past eighteen years we have worked with thousands of children helping them overcome the problems they encounter growing up. In our earlier book, *Good Behavior*, we shared our approach for improving behavior in ways that enable children and parents to feel better about themselves. The process and the techniques we developed work well for most children, but over the years we have become aware of a group of youngsters for whom these procedures are not enough. These children frustrate their teachers and tire their parents. Frequently labeled misunderstood, difficult, immature, hyperactive or attention deficit, these boys and girls look like other children, but their behavior separates them in a classroom or group. Often these youngsters are impulsive and hard to control. They have great difficulty focusing their attention, do not comply easily with rules, and often find it hard to sit still. The one thing you can count on with these youngsters is that they are unpredictable. Working with them and their families, we found ourselves challenged to devise special techniques, create support materials and develop different approaches until we found effective means to change their behavior.

As our special interest in children like these became known, more parents, teachers and pediatricians pressed us for our plan of action. How do you help a child stay on task? What do you do to increase self-control? How do you calm him down? What about his impulsiveness? Can you help her to get along better with other children? What should you tell the child and other family members? What do you think about medication? What is the best way to work with teachers and schools?

These may be your questions, too, or you may be drawn to this book for other reasons. You may wonder, "Is my son just 'all boy' or is he hyperactive?" Maybe it is your daughter's brief attention span that concerns you or the fact that your son rarely completes his schoolwork. Is he unmotivated or easily distractible? You may have heard the term *attention deficit disorder* (ADD) and question whether it applies to your child. Others of you know too well the answers to these questions and are struggling to find ways to help your child.

Whether you have read every book you can find on the subject or are just initiating your search for information, you are likely to be frustrated, anxious, maybe a little fearful. We understand your concerns. In recent years, there has been a great deal of publicity about hyperactivity and attention deficit disorders and an increasing number of books written about these topics. A good deal of conflicting information is presented as fact. Often, decisions about medication and diet are offered as the only direct choices a parent has to make.

In this book we intend to do much more than provide the background information necessary for you to understand your child's behavior. We will present the details of a treatment approach that can help you regain control of your situation. We will share our opinions and give you the answers that have worked so well for children like yours. We will lead you through the diagnostic process and help you orchestrate the information flow between your child's physician, psychologist, other professionals and your child's teachers. We will outline the techniques that can help increase your child's attention span, lengthen the time he sits with the family at the dinner table and permit him to "zap" the distractions that break his concentration. We will offer suggestions that will help you explain these problems to your child and gain for you the support of family and friends. We will clarify the issues about medication so you can make educated decisions about its appropriateness to your circumstances. And we will show you how to monitor the changes you seek to keep your progress headed in the right direction.

If Your Child Is Hyperactive, Inattentive, Impulsive, Distractible . . . is a home-based treatment program designed to be implemented by parents. It is a practical program that helps children build new behaviors. It is a program that requires your time and commitment. Accept the attitude that you and your child have years to learn together. Whether your child's behavior fits the classic definition of attention deficit hyperactivity disorder (ADHD) or he displays only a few of the characteristics of ADHD, elements of the program can help you deal more effectively with the behaviors that trouble you and hurt your child. Whether you begin on page one and continue until the conclusion or work on isolated behaviors, we will give you more options and present new techniques that will allow you to take control of your situation as your child gains control over his own behavior.

If Your
Child Is
Hyperactive,
Inattentive,
Impulsive,
Distractible . . .

Helping
the
ADD (Attention
. . . Deficit
Disorder)
Hyperactive
Child

1

My Child Has What?

*E*van, *five years old, is a slim, wiry perpetual-motion machine. He hardly stands, much less sits, still for more than a few moments from the time that he rises until he finally falls asleep late in the evening.*

Jessie is eight. You couldn't find a little girl with a sweeter face. She's adorable, with sandy blond hair cascading from two pigtails anchored with pink ribbons. Although rarely a troublemaker, she never finishes anything on time—her schoolwork, her food or getting dressed. She's a dreamer, creating castles in the sky.

Cal is fifteen with the body of a man, the swagger of a football player and the interests of a teenager. If a friend simply mentions an idea, Cal is going to do it. Without a thought or fear, he's in the

midst of any scheme. His teachers report that Cal is not an insti-
gator but the supreme reactor. He is so impulsive that his parents
worry he'll try drugs on a whim.

What do these youngsters have in common? At first glance, perhaps nothing. Yet in one major respect they are very similar. All have difficulty controlling some aspects of their behavior. For Evan it is movement—he cannot sit still. Jessie, Miss Personality to all who know her, remains a challenge to her parents and teachers. Not malicious or disrespectful, she simply never finishes anything. When it comes to Cal, the term impulsive could have been coined with him in mind.

Fidgeting, restlessness, interest in everything around them and tuning into one's own little world are behaviors common to every child at one time or another. What toddler is not a whirlwind in motion? Who has not known a teenager more fascinated by her own reveries than anything going on around her? And don't we all have to remind ourselves sometimes to think before we act or speak?

Most of us learn to focus on and accommodate to the world around us. Slowly but surely we master the rules and comply with them. What makes Evan, Jessie and Cal stand out so clearly among their peers is that their friends have begun to make these adjustments, but they have not. Just this issue may have brought you to this book—your fear that your child will not learn to adapt to the world around him. Will he eventually be able to sit through a meal? Will she ever get dressed fast enough to get to school on time or hold down a job? Is he going to be a sucker for every troublemaker? Will it be a constant struggle to get my child to adulthood?

We do not know when you first heard about attention deficits or hyperactivity and thought these might apply to your child. Some parents have compared their children to others for years, wondering if a lack of discipline caused their offspring to be so unruly and unreasonable. Other parents attribute their son's abundance of energy to the fact that he is a boy and do not think any more about it until the teacher calls that first time.

Everyone who reads this book has one overriding concern—

helping a child gain control over his own behavior, whether it is control over motion, mind or impulses.

Labels are important if they lead to a better understanding of your child. Even if a specific diagnosis is not appropriate, understanding attention deficits and hyperactivity may help you undertand your child's problems better.

In this chapter, we provide the background information that will clarify the terms that have been used to describe these problems including the most recent—attention deficit hyperactivity disorder (ADHD). Before we conclude the chapter we will summarize a variety of pet theories about what causes ADHD. Then with a common starting point, we will be ready to help you to define your child's specific problems and then help him.

■ *From BC to ADHD: The Evolution of the Term*

Organic driveness
Fidgety Phils
Postencephalitic behavior disorder
Minimal brain damage (MBD)
Minimal brain dysfunction (MBD)
Hyperkinesis
Hyperactivity
Attention deficit disorder (ADD)
Attention deficit disorder with or without hyperactivity
Attention deficit hyperactivity disorder (ADHD)

We do not know which term you first heard, but certainly these types of behavior problems are complicated enough without someone giving them a new name every five years. The word hyperactive has become so familiar that the abbreviated *hyper* crept into the vernacular some time ago. For the past ten years, ADD—attention deficit disorder—has been the preferred term. If you have only recently become comfortable with ADD, this may be your first introduction to ADHD—attention deficit hyperactivity disorder. Do not feel alone. We debated long and hard about which term to use in this book.

The accepted terminology has changed rapidly during the past fifty years. Unlike the latest automobile design, the alterations are not completely frivolous. Nor were they introduced to increase interest in the disorder. From hyperkinesis to hyperactivity, from attention deficit disorder and now to attention deficit hyperactivity disorder, these transitions reflect an increasing understanding of the condition.

Think back to your own school days. In every one of your classes there was probably at least one person who was the class clown or the daydreamer in the corner, who was rarely able to supply the right answer and who was often in trouble. Might that child have benefited from a diagnosis that would help his teachers to work more effectively with him?

Many labels are detrimental. Words like dunce, lazy and dumb always hurt, no matter who says them. Attention deficit hyperactivity disorder may not roll off your tongue, but as the term leads a parent, teacher, psychologist or physician to a better understanding of the child, it becomes less frightening and more useful.

Although at times you may feel totally alone as a parent dealing with a child who has ADHD characteristics, the research literature is full of descriptions of children like yours. As early as the late 1800s and continuing to the present, there are citations about restless, impulsive, overactive children who have difficulty concentrating. From organic driveness and postencephalitic behavior disorder to hyperkinesis and fidgety Phils, there have been at least twenty names applied in the twentieth century to describe children who have difficulty controlling various kinds of behavior.

Changes in terminology, though confusing to all of us, reflect the evolution of thought about the causes of this disorder and more recently, the relative importance of the symptoms. A strong trend through the years has been to force a medical model on the disorder. Medical scientists began studying the effects of brain injuries or illness on children's behavior during the nineteenth century. They noted that many patients who either survived an epidemic of encephalitis in the late 1800s or had had head injuries were hyperactive and had difficulty attending. Some researchers suggested that a diagnosis implying some degree of brain damage might also be a suitable explanation for children who had not been ill or hurt but who exhibited similar behaviors. Without conclusive evidence, the damage was assumed to be subtle.

Although the concept of some kind of minimal brain damage persisted as an explanation for these kinds of behaviors well into the 1940s, the notion remained difficult to defend. Many children who sustain brain injuries do not display hyperactive behaviors, and conversely, very few hyperactive children have any evidence of stuctural brain damage. Still convinced that neurological damage was the basis of these problems, researchers looked for "soft neurological signs" that could be considered evidence of brain dysfunction too subtle to be picked up by the diagnostic equipment available at the time. After finding a number of children who had trouble with fine or gross motor skills and difficulty imitating certain body movements that are standard parts of a neurological exam, the researchers felt it appropriate to amend the term minimal brain damage to minimal brain dysfunction. The formal name change to minimal brain dysfunction was made in 1966. Retaining the initials MBD reinforced an alphabet-soup mentality that led to years of confusion about the meaning of the term.

Somewhat ignored during this time was accumulating research indicating that one-half to two-thirds of children with concentration and activity problems did not fit the MBD pattern. Since the label remained popular, children with learning disabilities, attention problems, dyslexia, behavior disorders and hyperactivity were all at one time or another labeled MBD.

Also during the 1960s researchers shifted focus to look at the characteristics of the disorder rather than its causes. Using ingenious contraptions affectionately called "wiggle meters," studies were designed to measure what was assumed to be the excessive motion of these children. As hyperactivity crept innocuously into the jargon, new studies brought surprising results. These childen do not necessarily move more than other children, but they do have difficulty controlling their motion in situations that require stillness. Though the results demanded another swing in focus, they did provide another piece of this puzzle.

In the 1970s, Dr. Virginia Douglas and her colleagues at McGill University began demonstrating that it is difficult for hyperactive children to stop, look and listen, to sustain attention and to inhibit impulsivity. Others substantiated the notion that these children have problems controlling their behavior and adhering to rules. Furthermore, approximately 75 percent of the children were found to have additional learning disabilities.

Probably the only thing that is clear to you by now is that through the years there has been great confusion, and some ambiguity remains as professionals in a number of fields have attempted to define the significant characteristics of the condition. Naturally, this state of affairs has resulted in a wide variation in the professional advice proffered, making many educators and mental health specialists as well as parents uncomfortable.

Attempts to disentangle the terminology came when the American Psychiatric Association (APA) instituted the use of terms related to observed behavior to identify particular problems. When you visit a psychologist or psychiatrist, he designates the diagnosis for the visit just as your family physician does. These descriptors are defined in the *Diagnostic and Statistical Manual* of the American Psychiatric Association, which is the established diagnostic guide and reference tool used by mental health professionals.

In the second manual, *DSM-II*, published in 1968, the first term officially sanctioned for this collection of symptoms was hyperkinetic reaction of childhood (hyperactivity). When the role of concentration was recognized as central to the child's problems, then the effects of attentional deficits on learning and social interaction were given their due attention in the terminology. Thus, in the third *Diagnostic and Statistical Manual* of the APA, published in 1980, the complicated and somewhat clumsy label attention deficit disorder with or without hyperactivity was introduced.

Not only was attention deficit disorder with or without hyperactivity quite a mouthful but also, in hindsight, it may have placed an undue emphasis on the attentional aspects of the disorder, downplaying the impulsiveness and activity control problems these youngsters have. Although there are children with attention deficits who are not overly active, this is not the typical case. So again a revision was made in *DSM-III-R*, published in 1987.

Attempting to deal with the variation in patterns of behavior, *DSM-III-R* introduced the term attention deficit hyperactivity disorder (ADHD) and listed all the behaviors that characterize it. Since all children display one or all of these behaviors at some point in their lives, for a child to be diagnosed ADHD, eight or more of the symptoms, although varying in severity, must be noticeable for more than six months. Since ADHD is a developmental disorder, unless there is illness or injury, the onset of the symptoms must occur before a child is seven years old. The behaviors include:

1. restlessness
2. difficulty remaining seated when required to do so
3. easily distracted by extraneous stimuli
4. difficulty awaiting turn in games or group situations
5. often blurting out answers to questions before they have been completed
6. difficulty following instructions from others
7. difficulty sustaining attention in tasks or play activities
8. frequent shifts from one uncompleted activity to another
9. difficulty playing quietly
10. often talking excessively
11. often interrupting or intruding on other's games
12. often not seeming to listen to what is being said
13. often losing things
14. often engaging in physically dangerous activities without considering possible consequences

Based on this latest definition, what distinguishes the ADHD child from other children is the number of behaviors present, the length of time they continue and the degree to which they are evident. A single behavior, such as losing things, is irritating but meaningless unless it happens much more regularly than with your child's peers and coexists with many other of the critical behaviors. In addition, ADHD is not a condition that's present today and gone tomorrow. Although teachers are often the ones to recognize the significance of the behaviors, clues must have been apparent for a long time.

Regardless of the publicity and notoriety the disorder has received, only about 2 percent and at most 5 percent of the children in the United States meet the criteria for ADHD set forth in *DSM-III-R*. Based on these statistics, of every hundred students it is likely that two, three, or maybe as many as five could meet the criteria that designates ADHD. If true, it is even more predictable that those youngsters will be male because approximately nine times as many boys as girls are diagnosed ADHD. While there may not be hordes of ADHD children running around every neighborhood, when two of every hundred children have a particular set of problems, those numbers quickly add up.

■ *Everybody's Pet Theory*

There are likely to be a multitude of questions that have invaded your thoughts, and sleep, as you wonder:

"Why does my child have these problems?"
"Is it something we did as parents that caused him to be this way?"
"Could we have prevented it, or might we be contributing to it now?"

To alleviate your worst fears and to give you a summary of the best available information, we will answer the most frequent questions posed to us by parents of ADHD children.

There are many pet theories, some more promising than others, about what causes ADHD, but, just as the condition takes varying forms, several causes are likely. The research appears to be moving toward a growing consensus that ADHD has a biological base. Environmental conditions may play a role, too, especially in individual cases.

IS IT SOMETHING WE AS PARENTS DID OR DID NOT DO?

You have probably overheard the whispered accusations, "Why don't they do something about their child?" An endless stream of comments from grandparents, teachers and well-meaning friends can send any parent into the "guilts." True, some of us are better behavior managers than others, but then some children are easier to parent than others.

It is unlikely you are the cause of your child's behavior problems, but your child will indeed require more and different types of management than others. Many studies have been conducted to examine the interactions between mothers and their hyperactive children. Interactions between parent and child are reciprocal. Although you may strive to treat all your children the same, in reality that notion is impractical. When children do not follow instructions, parents normally become more directive, repeating the commands several times in a row. When the demands are not followed, both sets of behavior may intensify. The parent resorts to stronger actions to gain compliance. Several research studies by Drs. Russell Barkley and Charles Cunningham have shown that mothers of hyperactive children, probably as a result of their history of interactions, tend to become more negative, more directive and less responsive to the positive actions of their children. When their children's behavior improves because of medication or other interventions, mothers, having fewer negative interactions with their children, become less directive. When interacting with a nonhyperactive child, mothers of hyperactive children may be as positive as other mothers.

At times you no doubt have been so tired and frustrated by your child's behavior that you have wanted to give up, or perhaps you have blamed your child's behavior on your own inadequacies as a parent. Other parents experience the same feelings. You must remember ADHD is not a problem that can be totally cured, but as you will discover, many of the problems that accompany the disorder can be solved.

IS IT HEREDITARY?

Parents often have a striking reaction to a description of their child. "That sounds like me. You're describing the way I was as a child." Or after the last family reunion you may have wondered if Great-Uncle Melvin was the missing link.

It has become increasingly clear that the similarity between parent and child is not mere coincidence. Where children have been diagnosed as ADHD, retrospective studies searching the family histories of these individuals have found greater numbers of children and adults with behavioral characteristics of ADHD among family members. When the biological and adoptive families of ADHD children are compared, the correlation is between ADHD children and their biological families. A significantly greater number of ADHD biological siblings, for example, have the disorder than would be expected in the general population. The findings are most impressive if you consider that one-fourth of the biological parents of ADHD children, as opposed to only 4 percent of adoptive parents, also have histories indicative of ADHD.

While this research reflects a relatively small sample of families, many of the cases do suggest a genetic component to ADHD. If there are other well-defined cases of ADHD in your family, then there is reason to assume that your child's problems with restlessness and inattentiveness are inherited.

DID IT HAPPEN DURING BIRTH?

If there are no familial connections to your child's behavior and he has a very difficult birth history, then it's more likely but by no means certain that prenatal or perinatal complications may have contributed to this condition. While some evidence exists that damage to certain parts of the brain can lead to ADHD-like symptoms, many children with documented brain damage do not exhibit these kinds of behaviors. In fact, in several studies of children diagnosed as ADHD, only 5 to 10 percent had histories verifying brain damage. During the next decade, newer forms of brain study such as magnetic imaging may still detect evidence of more subtle brain dysfunction, if in fact birth factors do play a greater role in causing these symptoms.

IS IT CAUSED BY BRAIN DYSFUNCTION?

At least three different lines of research into brain activity appear to indicate a pattern of underactivity in certain areas of the brain that may explain why ADHD children show certain behaviors. The research that continues to accumulate suggests that ADHD children seem to have some kind of impairment of function in the cortical and subcortical areas of the brain. Drs. Arthur Anastopoulos and Russell Barkley summarized the research on neurological factors related to ADHD in 1988. For example, there are indications that ADHD children have decreased blood flow to the frontal lobes of the brain as indicated by decreased patterns of reactivity in their EEG wave patterns. More data stem from studies of the performance of ADHD children on neuropsychological tasks believed to be indicative of brain dysfunction. The last line of research involves the underarousal of the central nervous system in ADHD children. It has been hypothesized that cortical immaturity, as evidenced by electroencephalogram patterns, is the cause of inattention and impulsiveness. Conclusions from any of these areas of research are at best premature, because the limited number of studies and problems in comparing methodology prevent generalizations. However, research in brain activity appears to be an important direction for the future and may in fact lead to better understanding of ADHD symptoms.

IS IT CAUSED BY SOMETHING IN OUR CHILD'S DIET OR ENVIRONMENT?

If you knew you could correct or control ADHD by not allowing your child to eat a particular food substance or by keeping him away from certain substances, you would cut the offending substance from his diet or environment, wouldn't you? A great deal of research and an even greater interest on the part of parents has focused on the role of sugar, food additives and environmental toxins on the behavior of children.

In 1975, Dr. Benjamin Feingold suggested that more than half of all ADHD children display the characteristic behaviors because of adverse reactions to food additives. He claimed that if the parents limited the child's ingestion of those elements, the child's behavior would drastically improve. Many families tried this diet, but the results were mixed. Those whose children improved became wholehearted advocates of the diet. Despite individual reports, controlled research studies have not validated Feingold's theses. The same is also true of the popularly held beliefs that ingestion of refined sugars is the cause of hyperactive behavior. While there may be some children whose behavior is affected by the ingestion of particular food substances, this cannot account for the vast majority of ADHD children.

Exposure to toxins such as lead and nicotine or alcohol passed from mother to fetus during pregnancy have also come under increasing study in recent years and may account for some cases of ADHD. There are instances where certain anticonvulsant medications like phenobarbital and Dilantin have produced ADHD-like symptoms. Although evidence links ADHD-like symptoms to these substances, ultimately understanding how these substances affect the individual biologically will be more meaningful.

WAS HE JUST BORN THIS WAY?

Some researchers say ADHD is not a dysfunction or a deficit in the child, but part of the normal variation among human beings, such as differences in intelligence or height. Theoretically, if the height of every six-year-old child in the United States was measured and plotted on a graph, then the curve for heights would fall in a definite pattern with most of the children appearing in the average range and a lesser number at the taller and shorter ends of the graph (see Figure 1.1). Approximately 68 percent of the children's heights would cluster in the average range, but perhaps 2 percent of the children would be exceptionally short or extremely tall.

Some people believe that ADHD is another example of natural variation, like those which account for height and weight, intelligence, or artistic and athletic ability. According to this point of view, a study of a population would find across individuals a range of temperaments and attention spans. Such a distribution of traits and behaviors reflects human variation and normal development. According to this way of thinking, even though heredity plays a role, your child was just born that way; your child's behavior represents various points on a continuum of possibilities.

If you apply this approach, in a typical classroom, most children will have an average attention span. There will be a few

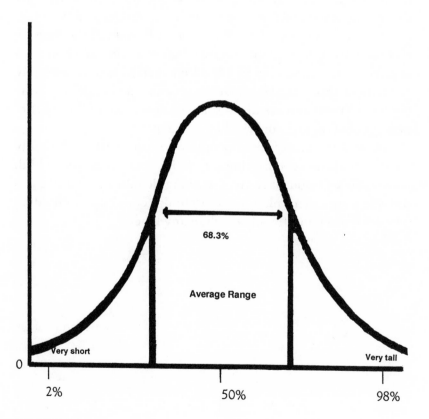

FIGURE 1.1
The Normal Curve

children who can concentrate "all day long" and not be distracted by anything short of a bulldozer coming through the
classroom. On the other end of the continuum, there will be a
few children whose attention span is so brief, they are distracted by the color of the walls. This point of view may explain
why some children who have no family or birth history suggesting ADHD are the way they are.

In this chapter we have attempted to clarify some of the
issues and present a working definition of the term ADHD.
Working is the key word. The greatest consensus about ADHD is
that it represents a collection of symptoms and a range of behaviors. At the same time that your child may be very impulsive, have a short attention span and be less active than his
sibling, another child may be very distractible, highly active
and have a short attention span—yet both could fit the diagnosis of ADHD. While a label implies that everyone to whom it is
applied is the same, keep in mind that such an idea is definitely
not true of this disorder. Make no mistake, no one should hear
the label ADHD and assume he or she knows your child's particular set of symptoms or why he has them.

You and the professional people who work with your family
must define the specific characteristics that affect your child.
Only then will you have the "working definition" you need to
provide a treatment plan for your child. Your child's individual
problems are more important than any label.

2
■

How to Tell If Your Child Really Has ADHD

*W*hen your child has an acute sore throat, a pain or a rash, you take him to the family doctor, who probes with educated hands and identifies the cause. Then, just as capably, the physician prescribes a remedy for the problem, which typically works—sooner or later.

Your life, and ours, would be so much simpler if there was one test that would accurately pinpoint ADHD, followed by a simple treatment. Unfortunately no such single measure or remedy exists.

Like many other behavioral disorders, ADHD is very complex. There are similarities among children who are diagnosed as having ADHD, but there are also huge differences. Two children may overlap in some symptoms but diverge greatly in others. The severity of characteristics displayed by individual children varies greatly, making an instant diagnosis virtually impossible. The symptoms may not be apparent in the doctor's office or in any one-to-one situation, yet be immediately visible in other situations. One child may be extremely hyperactive; another fairly quiet, but highly distractible; and a third child may not display any severe symptoms, but still be moderately affected by impulsivity, distractibility and overactivity.

Diagnosis is not an all-or-none proposition and definitely not as clearcut as finding out that your child's fever is due to an earache. A diagnosis of ADHD requires the coordinated efforts of several professionals asking the right questions and using a variety of tests to eliminate problems that mimic ADHD.

In this chapter we will lead you through the steps that should be included in diagnosing ADHD, eliminate as many mysteries as possible, identify the professionals who might be involved, and present questions you will want to ask along the way.

■ *Early Warning Signs of ADHD*

The diagnostic process may have begun with you. When did you have that first hunch there might be another explanation for your child's behavior? The recurrent behavior patterns of some toddlers lead their parents to suspect the child has some sort of problem very early, but for any number of reasons, a final diagnosis may not come until years later.

With the increased publicity ADHD has received, parents more familiar with the disorder begin to speculate about the problem much earlier. It is not at all unusual for a parent of a two-year-old or an infant to inquire whether it is too early to diagnose ADHD. Years ago most inquiries came after a child first entered school. Parents are now much more sophisticated about potential problems and are less reluctant to seek professional advice for their children.

The experiences of Evan's parents illustrate many of the early characteristics noticed by parents of an ADHD child. Even before her child was born, Evan's mother thought he was unusually active. More than merely kicking, he seemed to be roaming in the womb. Although the experience contrasted with that of her first pregnancy, Mom chalked this up to the fact that her second baby was a boy. In fact, his maleness received much of the blame for Evan's excessive activity. When he climbed out of the crib, his coordination and dexterity were attributed to the fact that he was a boy. As a toddler, when he continually "got into everything," it was because he was "all boy." And when he had difficulty going to sleep and seemed to need very little rest, it was because Dad roughhoused with the little guy.

The combination of trying to maintain a work load, keep up with Evan in the daytime, and manage on very little sleep themselves frazzled both parents. Finally, in a desperate attempt safely to contain their child at night, they put a latch on Evan's bedroom door. Imagine their horror when they discovered their four-year-old son had climbed out the window and was riding his tricycle on the front walk at five A.M. Evan did not calm down over time. By age five, two preschools had strongly suggested that he might be better served by other programs.

There are not many children who are so clearly hyperactive as Evan, but his story does depict a number of the symptoms many children who are later diagnosed with ADHD have in common. Since these children do not seem to require much sleep, bedtime and naptime become constant battles. When they do sleep, they toss and turn, twisting the bedsheets into a pile of knots.

These children are never quite still. First they try to climb out of their high chairs. Perched in a real chair, they wiggle and rock until the moment they are out of the seat altogether. In play, they wander from toy to toy, only temporarily entertained.

On the other hand, a child like this can be enthralled by the television, rhythmically bouncing or frozen in front of the beloved screen so that the rest of his surroundings appear to fade away. Other favorite activities such as drawing or building with tiny blocks may also hold him spellbound for long periods, but as a rule, his attention lasts something closer to a few minutes.

There are other perplexing contrasts with these youngsters. Although they may have been early climbers, walkers or runners, frequently these kids are so noticeably clumsy that they wear bruises and bumps like badges across their bodies. Many parents are embarrased by the number of times they must make unscheduled trips to the doctor or emergency room. These accidents have more to do with rashness than awkwardness. These children simply tend to leap before they look, with little or no thought to the consequences of their actions.

Most parents of ADHD youngsters immediately recognize their own child from such descriptions, or at least from portions of them. There are, however, children who present a very different set of characteristics who also show early signs of an attention deficit. Some babies and toddlers are so underactive they are labeled hypoactive. Much of their time is spent sitting contentedly holding a toy, neither staring nor playing with it. With only fleeting interest in anything new, they appear almost unaware of what is going on around them. When they do attempt to retrieve an item they are bound to be sidetracked by an endless number of distractions that would scarcely draw anyone else's notice. As they get older, questions about "Why didn't you do what I asked?" are met with that blank stare that drives parents up the wall.

The disturbing behaviors parents first recognize are often those noted frequently in histories of children later diagnosed as having problems with attention or hyperactivity. Compiling these behavior characteristics, we have developed a list of early warning signs for ADHD children. Use the Early Warning Checklist presented on page 21 to review your child's behavior.

A child who has ADHD may match the descriptions completely or have only a few of the symptoms. On the other hand, the fact that your child's behavior corresponds to a few of the items in the list does not complete a diagnosis. Probably most of the children who exhibit selective attention to a parent's requests or who are occasionally entranced by the television or a video game are not ADHD. This is one time when comparisons with other children of the same age and sex can help you make the distinction. Observations of your child playing with peers in an organized activity, at a play group or at preschool, can provide relevant information. Be aware, though, that initial shyness or excitement can magnify traits that fade once a child is comfortable with the rest of the individuals involved and the situation. Preschool teachers who have had experience with many different children are a valuable resource for you.

There is no score for our checklist, but the more items to which you answer yes or the more strongly your child demonstrates a particular behavior, the more likely that behavior may be an early sign of ADHD. The checklist will help guide your observations of your child provided he is below the age of five, whereas if your child is already in school, think back to what he was like as a toddler.

EARLY WARNING CHECKLIST

____1. Was your child much more active in the womb than his siblings?

____2. Did your child have trouble establishing a normal sleep pattern, and does he still require much less sleep than his siblings or same-age peers?

____3. Is your child much more squirmy than his peers, especially in situations that require him to sit still, such as at mealtimes, when riding in the car, when sitting in restaurants?

____4. Does your child switch from activity to activity more quickly than the average child his age? For example, does he have trouble playing with most toys for as long as designed or in the manner a peer would?

____5. Does your child normally have trouble taking turns or waiting for the simplest request to be fulfilled, such as getting him a drink?

____6. Is your child not just a climber but a constant scaler who ends up on top of things and in places other children only dream of but wouldn't dare try to reach? Has he ever gotten onto the top of the refrigerator, been stuck in a tree or climbed onto the roof?

____7. Is your child a daydreamer who looks at you with blank stares as you talk to him?

■ *Medical Exams*

When a child continues to show signs of impulsivity, distractibility and/or hyperactivity, then the first formal step in diagnosis is to discuss your concerns with your pediatrician or family physician. A number of physical problems that look like ADHD should be ruled out before a true diagnosis of a primary attentional disorder is made. Many of these conditions are rare, but that makes it all the more important to eliminate them before proceeding. If they are present, you will want to treat them immediately. Many of the things your pediatrician or family physician will be looking for are discussed in this section.

THYROID DISEASE

The thyroid is a small gland located in the throat near the Adam's apple," or larynx, which regulates many important body functions, including metabolism. Either an overactive or underactive thyroid gland can cause symptoms that emulate ADHD.

A condition called hyperthyroidism induces this gland to overproduce hormones, causing the body to speed up. As a result a person may feel jittery and appear restless, much like an individual who is hyperactive.

If the thyroid produces an inadequate amount of hormone, this can lead to a condition called hypothyroidism. When this occurs, a person's metabolism may slow down, causing him to gain weight and feel sluggish. The individual may appear to daydream, be distractible or to tune others out. It would not be at all surprising if he had trouble remaining alert during sedentary activities.

By examining your child, a physician can detect signs of an extreme problem. Otherwise a blood test routinely included in most physical exams will be used to determine if there is a thyroid-related problem.

HEARING PROBLEMS

As a practical observation, over the years we have noticed a correlation between children referred to us because they were not paying attention in class and a history of chronic ear infections. These same children had often passed the brief auditory screening conducted at school with flying colors, because certain kinds of hearing weaknesses are not immediately apparent in that setting. Only a specialist has the necessary equipment to detect hearing losses of particular frequencies and at various decibel readings that may be permanent or temporary.

A child who is subject to frequent ear infections may have congestion in the middle ear that impedes hearing. There are fluctuations in this condition, explaining how it happens that a child with frequent ear infections may appear to pay attention well one day and not another. These losses may also provide partial explanations for why such children show gaps in language knowledge, affecting the child's ability not only to produce sounds and understand certain syntactic structures but also to develop vocabulary.

Sometimes children who have these kinds of problems concentrate better when they take antihistamines. Do not confuse this with the assumption that the child would also respond to medication for ADHD; it is more likely the child attends better because his hearing has improved as a result of the medication.

ALLERGIES AND UPPER RESPIRATORY ILLNESSES

There has been a great deal of controversy over whether allergies are the cause of attentional problems. Dr. Ben Feingold was one of the leading proponents of the theory that hyperactivity and attentional deficits are caused by allergies to food additives. Others believe that sugar is the primary culprit. To date, no conclusive scientific evidence in any large sample of children has been found to support the theory that food reactions cause ADHD symptoms. There are parental and clinical reports of particular children being affected by such factors, but research shows it is highly unlikely that this is the source of these symptoms for the vast majority of ADHD children.

On the other hand, a number of children who have attentional problems are allergic to airborne substances. These kinds of allergies can affect a child's concentration. When a child has several periods of time each year during which he is congested, has difficulty breathing, and spends his time blowing his nose or sniffling, his concentration during the day and his sleep at night are both being frequently interrupted. Consequently the youngster is likely to feel tired and less energetic and therefore less tuned in to what is going on around him.

Many children we see for assessment are noticeably more distractible and restless on days when they are suffering with stuffy noses and watery eyes. Not only do they look ill but their performance is affected as well. With a little detective work, one may discover a pattern of less successful school performance that corresponds to the seasons of the child's allergic reactions.

Unfortunately, diagnosis and treatment for allergies alone do not always remedy the situation. Sometimes allergy treatment complicates the situation. Breathing may ease with treatment, but a number of medications commonly prescribed to open airways have side effects that interfere with concentration. Some prescription drugs and over-the-counter remedies may cause a child to become agitated or drowsy so that concentrating in the classroom is very difficult.

NEUROLOGICAL PROBLEMS

Sometimes a child's problems attending may be caused by neurological problems. On rare occasions a child's blank stare into space may be indicative of a very small, or petit mal, seizure. These are brief periods during which the child is totally unaware of his surroundings and afterwards may be unable to recall what occurred. As brief as a few seconds to as long as a minute or more, these episodes are so dissimilar to what people usually think of as a seizure that they easily pass unnoticed. The child does not fall to the ground and his eyes do not roll back into his head. There is no danger of the child swallowing his tongue, but a youngster experiencing a petit mal seizure will have a glassy stare, perhaps blink rapidly and may not respond to questions. Afterwards, the youngster rarely complains, for he tries to hide the fact he does not know what he missed or even why.

If you suspect this may be happening to your child, discuss it with your pediatrician or family physician. Your doctor will probably ask to observe your child and may want him to touch his fingertips together quickly or balance on one foot. A child's inability to complete these physical tasks is considered to be a soft sign or evidence of a neurological problem. To complete the workup your doctor may advise that a specialist conduct further neurological testing, including an EEG (electroencephalogram), to reveal any brain wave patterns indicative of underlying seizure activity. Do not panic if some abnormal brain wave activity is revealed. The degree of abnormality is the important factor. Your physician will explain whether the pattern is one that may lead to more full seizure activity. Fortunately, most childhood seizure disorders can be controlled by medication (not the same ones used for ADHD), and often children outgrow such problems.

■ Parent Questionnaires

As a parent, you have had a unique opportunity to observe your child in a variety of situations; you have the advantage of living with him day in and day out. Clearly, you have a good deal of information about your child that is important in the diagnostic process. The problem is how to organize that information in ways that will be helpful to the professionals who are working with your family.

A physician, psychologist or other professional can ask questions, but without a means of determining if the characteristics you describe are typical or "normal" for children your child's age, they will not be able to attach a meaning to any discernible patterns. If it is virtually impossible for any two-year-old to sit quietly at a desk for five minutes, then the fact that your child cannot accomplish this feat is not unusual. If your two-year-old regularly sleeps a total of five hours a night as compared to twice that amount for most toddlers, then that fact becomes significant.

To accumulate data on typical childhood behavior patterns and those of children who have ADHD, psychologists have asked thousands of parents to complete a series of questions about their children's behavior. Most of the questions relate to the way children act and respond in typical childhood situations at home and elsewhere. To validate the information collected through these questionnaires, comparisons were made between the answers parents gave and direct observations of the children. The result is a series of parent questionnaires that can be used to compare your child's behavior with that of other children the same age.

When completing a parent questionnaire, each parent should answer the questions individually. If you like, afterwards you may compare answers with your spouse, but do not change your responses.

While the number of forms parents are asked to complete can be a bit overwhelming initially, the information gathered is significant. The process can be surprisingly enlightening. Parents may discover that they have drastically different views of their child's behavior. These contradictions may be disturbing to parents, but awareness of such discrepancies may help pinpoint differences in attitude, perspective or approach within a household. The professionals working with you can then use the questionnaires as tools to plan unified treatment strategies.

You and your spouse can go over your individual answers yourselves. Instead of trying to convince each other of a particular point of view, discuss the item, attempting to figure out why each of you rated the child as you did. In the process you may arrive at a new point of agreement about how to deal with a particular situation and clearer rules about key problems that concern you.

There are a number of commonly used questionnaires. We shall discuss several of these so that you will be familiar with these elements of the diagnostic process.

WERRY-WEISS-PETERS ACTIVITY RATING SCALE (W.W.P.A.R.S.)

Werry-Weiss is one of the easiest questionnaires for parents to use. It contains twenty-two questions about the child's behavior in a number of different situations, including mealtime, while watching TV, playtime, bedtime/sleeping, and in public. Applicable to children ages three to nine, the questions focus on activity. The information about concentration, distractibility or impulsiveness is extremely limited, but the instrument has been shown to be sensitive to improvements in behavior due to medication or behavior therapy. Werry-Weiss is best used as one of several screening devices to determine if a young child's behavior falls in the hyperactive range. If both you and your spouse have a high score and agree about your child's activity level in most of the situations, then these results increase the likelihood that your child may be hyperactive.

CONNERS PARENT RATING SCALE (CPRS)

The Conners questionnaire, developed by C. Keith Conners, Ph.D., is probably the most widely used of all parent questionnaires for ADHD. Over the years, many studies have been conducted showing its effectiveness in distinguishing between ADHD youngsters and those who do not have this disorder. The forty-eight-question version yields scores on a number of problems including conduct disorder, anxiety, learning problems, psychosomatic symptoms, impulsivity/hyperactivity, and a hyperactivity index. Although the questionnaire has been criticized as too limited in the number of items related to anxiety and pure attentional deficits apart from hyperactivity, it is a helpful measure when considered as part of a complete diagnostic package. There are also brief parent and teacher forms in the Conners questionnaire that have been shown to be sensitive to changes in a child's behavior and that are easy to use for monitoring behavior.

HOME SITUATION QUESTIONNAIRE (HSQ)

The HSQ, developed by Dr. Russell Barkley, is another relatively easy-to-use instrument that can help to distinguish typical from ADHD behavior patterns. The questionnaire lists sixteen different situations for which the parent indicates whether or not the child has problems and if so, how severe. If a child has high ratings in seven or more areas, his behavior probably parallels that of ADHD youngsters.

This questionnaire is most useful to a clinician as an indicator of where a child's problems occur most often. Since these ratings cannot directly measure activity level or attention span, a child may score high on this scale because he has behavior problems not ADHD.

■ *Teacher Ratings*

Just as you have been in a distinct position to watch your child over the years, so too have his teachers, particularly in regard to a child's attentional abilities. They have seen him attempt to concentrate on a variety of tasks and noticed how much his environment and the students in it distract him. If a child is impulsive, rushes to begin tasks before the instructions are complete, blurts out answers to questions and finds it nearly impossible to wait his turn, it is obvious to the teacher. On the playground, overactivity is not immediately apparent, but once a child enters the classroom, he must sit down.

A teacher also has the advantage of a comparison group. Having taught school for a number of years, a teacher has worked with many students. In your child's classroom, in front of her eyes are other children offering an immediate comparison. The contrast among behaviors is obvious. A number of research studies have found that teachers' ratings on various scales may be the best predictors of which children are ADHD. The more of your child's teachers who rate him as ADHD, the greater the likelihood that the child really has an attention deficit.

CONNERS TEACHER RATING SCALE (CTRS)

Probably the best known and most widely used teacher questionnaire, the CTRS consists of twenty-eight questions that yield scores on four factors: conduct problems, hyperactivity, inattention-passivity, and a hyperactivity index. This instrument is more sensitive than the parent's form of the Conners to differences between hyperactive children and those who are not. When a child's teachers complete the questionnaire, the comparison of their observations has proved to be a significant source of information for the diagnosis of ADHD. The teacher rating scale also appears to reflect the effects of medication or behavioral interventions on a child's behavior.

■ *Other Questionnaires*

There are a number of other teacher questionnaires. The Child Behavior Checklist (CBCL) by T. M. Achenbach is composed of 112 questions. In regard to each behavior described, the teacher responds not true of the child, somewhat or sometimes true, or very true, very often. When scored, this instrument yields ratings on anxiety, depression, aggressiveness, delinquency, withdrawal, obsessiveness and somatic complaints as well as hyperactivity. The value of this measure is that it sorts out a variety of reasons why a child may be acting in a particular manner. For example, if the child is very anxious and acting compulsively, it will affect his concentration. The CBCL does a much better job of defining emotional and behavioral factors than does the Conners.

The ADD-H Comprehensive Teacher's Rating Scale (ACTeRS) is another new scale that primarily focuses on characteristics of attention deficits and hyperactivity. The questions completed by the teacher seem as effective as the Conners in measuring hyperactivity, but may be more accurate in delineating ADD without the hyperactive component.

■ *Psychological Evaluations*

The notion of taking your child to a psychologist for testing, though, is not obscure, cryptic, romantic, mystical, or miraculous—and it shouldn't be frightening. Psychological evaluation is a very straightforward and routine process. From your child's point of view, he will be drawing, completing puzzles, answering some questions, and performing a variety of tasks that look similar to the ones his teachers ask him to do at school.

During their time together, the psychologist will work with your child not only to obtain measures of intellectual potential and achievement but also to gain some indication of the child's emotional well-being. These sessions provide many opportunities for the psychologist to observe how your child reacts to frustration, how long he is able to sustain his attention and concentration, and how he responds to time constraints. By means of interviews, paper-and-pencil tests, and direct observations, the psychologist will evaluate how anxious your child is, what his overall level of happiness seems to be, and what his self-concept is in terms of school, family and friends. Other emotional factors that might be affecting him will also be explored. Psychoeducational testing should also identify any learning disabilities or processing problems that make it difficult for your child to complete work or stay on task.

As a result of psychoeducational testing, you should be able to find out whether your child is overachieving, underachieving or doing work at the appropriate level for his ability. Your child's need to achieve and his level of motivation will also be considered, even though these are not exact measures. Finally, the psychologist may use a number of methods, including several computerized tasks like those included in the Gordon Diagnostic System, to assess attention span, concentration, distractibility and impulsiveness.

You might assume that from this collection of information an exact diagnosis can be made. Unfortunately, psychology is not a science that yields isolated results. To draw any conclusions about whether ADHD is part of or all of your child's problem, the specialist must interpret the scores of the psychoeducational tests in terms of everything else that is known about your child. No psychological exam exists to diagnose ADHD definitively. In fact, many youngsters are able to sit still and concentrate quite well throughout an entire psychological assessment but are incapable of maintaining that same stance in a noisy classroom full of distractions.

■ *Pulling It All Together*

You have visited the specialists; your child has taken the tests, been examined and observed; you have answered the questions and completed the forms. Quite a lot of information has been compiled about your child. Most of the time the long-awaited simple "Yes, he has it" or "No, he doesn't" is not forthcoming and may not suffice anyway. Someone must sift through the data, determine the diagnosis and plan a course of action. Frequently, one of the professionals takes charge, but in many instances you will need to assume an active role in coordinating the communication between the various experts.

By now you have a collection of reports and results. Read the reports carefully with marker in hand. Highlight those parts that don't make sense to you or the conclusions that conflict with each other or your own assessments of your child's behavior. Then compose your questions and get ready to direct them to the appropriate professional. It is always more efficient to collect your questions for each specialist in advance. Some parents worry that their questions will appear foolish. There is no need to worry about that; your questions reflect your concern, and that is what counts.

As you discuss the results, speak up. Point out the inconsistencies you see, asking each professional for an opinion. Prompt each specialist to talk with others who have been involved in the diagnostic process until the contradictions are resolved and a final diagnosis is made.

You must be aware that your child's age will be a factor in diagnosis. While it is always better to discover problems as early as possible, particular difficulties come into focus only as a child develops. Except in the case of the most hyperactive children, assessing attentional deficits is hard to do in the very young child. If a child's weaknesses are mild or due to several factors, it may be hard for any professional to draw a definite conclusion. Even when you understand the diagnostic process, sometimes you will not get the definitive answer you seek. Use the information you do receive to pinpoint the various causes of your child's attentional problems.

We have developed the diagnostic checklist below that will help you pull the information you have gathered into usable form.

MEDICAL *(Be sure to discuss this with your physician.)*

___1. Does your child have any medical problems that may in any way affect his ability to sustain attention?

___2. Do any of the medications your child takes for any condition have side effects that could interfere with concentration or memory?

___3. Does your child have vision or hearing problems that would make it difficult for him to follow directions, comprehend oral instructions or do written work?

___4. Does your child ever stare into space and have lapses in memory about what just occurred?

___5. Does your child have frequent headaches?

___6. Is your child clumsy or more accident-prone than children his age?

PSYCHOLOGICAL

___1. Does your child show signs of nervousness or anxiety? Some signs to look for are nail biting, or other nervous habits, cold sweaty palms, upset stomach before tests, excessive worrying, trembling or other overt signs of being tense.

___2. Did the psychologist or learning specialist note signs of excessive anxiety during testing? Did your child's performance on psychological or educational tests or any ratings completed by teachers or parents indicate excessive anxiety, depression or conduct problems that could be the primary disrupters of concentration?

___3. Did testing reveal that your child is preoccupied with other thoughts that could be blocking him from attending? Is he worried about making or keeping friends, achieving in school or getting along with peers and siblings?

____**4.** Are there conflicts or other problems occurring within the family that may cause your child to be worried or depressed?

____**5.** Is your child frequently angry or at times aggressive?

EDUCATIONAL

____**1.** Did your child's testing reveal deficits in particular skills, such as reading, math or other subject areas? Are those gaps large enough to make it difficult for your child to complete his work in a reasonable amount of time without frustration?

____**2.** Did testing indicate any processing problems or learning disabilities that interfere with your child's acquiring new learning, retrieving old information or expressing what he already knows orally or in writing?

____**3.** Can your child listen and follow directions at the level they are given in the classroom? Does he need instructions broken down and repeated before he is able to correctly start a task?

____**4.** At his current class placement, is your child able to keep up with his peers academically? Does he compare himself only to the best students in each subject area so that he feels inferior?

BEHAVIOR/ATTENTION

____**1.** How many of the parent and teacher ratings yielded results that were significant for
____ hyperactivity
____ short attention span
____ impulsiveness
____conduct problems

____**2.** Did direct observations of your child by an independent rater find a high incidence of off-task behavior during class time?

Diagnosis is not an end. While many of us prefer the security of labels and statistics, the results are important only if they lead to help for a child. Whether your child fits the diagnosis of ADHD or not, he displays behaviors that trouble you—impulsivity, distractibility, inattentiveness or overactivity. The remainder of this book will be about how you can help your child with each aspect of his problem.

3
.

Motivating Your Child

When a child has trouble sitting still, staying on task or controlling his impulses, the natural tendency is to punish his outbursts, correct his off-task behavior and still his motion. Although these actions may succeed momentarily, the effects of punishment are usually transient. Though temporarily suppressed, difficult behaviors, like weeds, spring back up as soon as the negative consequences pass. The parent feels defeated; the child does, too. This punishment cycle is repeated many times each day with the ADHD child, but there is another way to motivate your child to learn to change.

Ninety-nine percent of the children we ask "What is discipline?" quickly respond, "Punishment." What comes to your mind? The classic definition of discipline is teaching or training for appropriate behavior. With this view of discipline comes a new orientation to your job as a parent. Rather than looking for and stamping out undesirable behaviors, you turn your focus to nurturing the positive behaviors your child displays and teaching new behaviors to replace the problem ones, which results in more lasting change. In the process, your child gathers motivation to change.

This is the approach we advocate for all children, parents and teachers, but it is even more crucial for youngsters who have ADHD characteristics. Changing a behavior always involves hard work. It will take hard work to help your child change the problem behaviors that hinder him now. It will take time, too. No parent should expect to see immediate permanent change. Working parents and even those with more time must adopt a new attitude and a long-term view of progress. Like the tortoise you have time to help your child. Over the years, your effort will pay off as your child builds positive behaviors to replace the old ones.

You will see this approach employed throughout this book. It is reflected in the chapter titles: Stretching Attention Span, Controlling Activity Level, Beating Distractions, Following Rules. Each chapter presents a new set of techniques your child will learn. In this chapter we will explain some very important principles that will help to increase your child's motivation.

■ Positive Principles

First, *pick one problem at a time*. It is easy to get overwhelmed. If you were to attempt to work simultaneously on all of the aspects of ADHD demonstrated in this book, you and your child would burn out before a week was through. Instead, focus on one of your child's problems. Follow the suggestions in the appropriate chapter and stick with them until you have made significant progress. Then continue to another area.

Start with the basics. If your child has trouble sitting still, you must begin with the exercises in Chapter 7 before you can go on to other aspects of the training, such as beating distractions. If your child is not hyperactive, you may still choose to begin with calmness training since the relaxation techniques suggested here often enhance learning in other areas. Concentrating your energy on one aspect of your child's problems makes the project doable. Meeting with some success will increase the motivation to tackle other areas.

Even when you focus on one problem, you must think small and *look for small steps toward success*. Many times your child's success will be measured in seconds, sitting for a few seconds longer, working for a few additional seconds on a homework task, or waiting a few seconds longer to respond. During a period of days and weeks those seconds will increase in number, and the small steps toward success will add up. Setting realistic goals and working toward them one second, one minute or one step at a time can lead to sustained progress.

We are not Pollyannas. It would be wonderful if all progress were achieved through positive means, but learning often requires both positive and negative consequences. Even so, you will find we talk much more about praising and rewarding children for learning and using new behaviors than we do about negative consequences. We have found *it takes more positive than negative consequences to teach new behavior patterns to a child.* Positive consequences are also more effective in encouraging a child to replace old behavior patterns with new ones.

Before reading any further, record on a form such as the one shown in Figure 3.1 the next ten comments you make to your child. For each statement, define it as a positive comment, a criticism, or a direction. "Pick up your books" is a direction; "Don't pick on your sister" is a criticism; and "Thank you for waiting for me to get off the phone" is a positive comment.

What percentage of your feedback was negative or directive versus positive? A number of research studies indicate that parents of ADHD children correct and direct their children more often than parents of non-ADHD children. It is a learned response. In an effort to manage and control your child, you too may have become more negative than you would like. When your child is overactive, is easily stimulated and does not follow rules, when you are exhausted from trying to manage him, it is very easy to recognize only the negative aspects of a child's behavior.

One youngster said, "I have an attention deficit . . . I don't get enough attention!" Though children seek attention, the question is what kind of attention they receive. Your child wants your attention more than anything else. The key is when and how you give attention.

HOW POSITIVE AM I?		
Positive Comment	Criticism	Direction
1.		
2.		
3.		
4.		
5.		
6.		
7.		
8.		
9.		
10.		

FIGURE 3.1
Record of Verbal Statements

We have a rule of thumb you will find helpful. If you correct your child for a negative behavior, try to praise him four or more times for doing something right before he has the chance to misbehave again. You may think this is impossible, but you will be surprised to discover how many positive opportunities pass without comment during the day. If your child sits down between jumps, plays quietly for a minute, asks an appropriate question, puts his napkin in his lap, waits his turn in a game, hangs a towel on the bath rod, each act represents an occasion to praise him. There are numerous positive behaviors that escape notice every day.

When you praise your child, avoid "good boy" or "good girl" comments. Such praise can backfire. If your child thinks, "Now they expect me always to be good . . . I can't do that," it will rob him of his motivation to seek more realistic goals.

Give specific positive feedback about what your child does right. By saying, "I like the way you sat in the chair with your feet on the floor," you provide the child with information about what he did correctly and how pleased you are. "You should feel very good about the way you helped your sister complete the puzzle" also asks the child to accept responsibility for this behavior. Effective positive feedback gives the child credit for a behavior and motivates the child to take the same actions again.

One technique we find very helpful to increase the overall level of positive feedback is a good behavior diary. Using a simple spiral notebook dedicated to this purpose, record everything in the book your child does right. Tell him, "That's one for the book!" as you record a description of what he did. For the older child a wink or a private notation may be preferred. At first, review the entries in the diary with your child every day. Later, space them over longer periods of time. If your spouse travels or returns home several days a week after your children are asleep, set regular times to review the list. This will short-circuit the old bad-news pattern of "Wait until your father (or mother) gets home. . . ." When Mom or Dad is out of town, sharing the good behavior book with the traveling spouse keeps him or her apprised of the positive activity at home.

In addition to praise and attention, we believe in the special use of rewards to establish new behaviors. Throughout our first book, *Good Behavior*, and this one, we discuss using various charts and a point system to motivate children to succeed. We realize that many parents have tried rewards or used elaborate point systems, tracking fourteen different behaviors with complicated exchange rates for each. Often the parents and the child become frustrated and discouraged by programs that require the youngster to perform for an entire week or more before earning any kind of a reward. Frequently the initial motivational value of the points fades before the desired behavior change is met. This leads many to conclude that rewards do not work or are not worth the trouble. Other parents avoid rewards because they do not like the idea of paying their children to behave appropriately and fear bargaining for good behavior will be an ongoing struggle.

■ *Effective Reinforcement*

A reinforcement system should be very simple. If you follow these rules you will use rewards properly and avoid the pitfalls you fear.

Use rewards to get a new behavior going. Once that behavior is established, you will wean your child from the rewards while maintaining the new standard of behavior.

Focus all of your rewards on one or at most two related behaviors at a time. If you are teaching your child how to sit still, then that should be the focus of all your efforts. Later on, in Chapter 7, sitting still will be given a context, such as sitting at the dinner table and using the appropriate utensils. This approach permits you to shape your child's behavior so that you build more complex sets of behaviors and avoid rewarding every single thing your child does.

Give a small immediate reward and points that accumulate for a longer-term reward. In the beginning, your child's earning power should have a dual nature. The first time your child cooperates in learning a new strategy give him an immediate reward. It can be a sticker, an opportunity to select a prize from a grab bag of trinkets you have collected or some other small reward. In addition let your child earn points toward a larger reward that he will be able to "buy" at a later time.

Do not make the mistake initially of letting your child select an expensive item that requires the accumulation of many points over an extended period of time. To prevent a child from becoming discouraged and to keep his motivation high, it is important that he redeem points frequently. Since he must spend all of his points once each goal is met, a child will be regularly exchanging points for smaller items, privileges and activities that can be earned in a few days. Gradually as a behavior builds, your child should have the opportunity to work for larger rewards that take longer to earn.

For this plan to be most effective, children need to see the points they are earning accumulate. You might use plastic tokens or poker chips saved in a glass container if you like. We have adopted a paper-and-pencil system of totaling points because it can be maintained anywhere and you will never run out of chips.

The First National Bank of Points is shown in Figure 3.2. Using this chart your child fills in increasing parts of the bank as he earns additional points. Each point is represented as a number. As it is spent, the number is crossed out and a new series is started. Another form of this bank is shown in Figure 7.3 in Chapter 7.

At first make it easy to earn a reward in just a few days. Figure 3.3 depicts Jim's bank. Jim, who is five years old, earned a free reach into a grab bag his mother filled and a point to deposit in his point bank each time he sat in his chair for the specified goal. When he accumulated three points for sitting in his chair at the dinner table, he exchanged them for a reward. Since he spent all of his points, Jim was eager to work toward a new goal.

Your child should be able to exchange his points for a reward within a reasonable period of time. The younger the child, the shorter the time delay can be. In the beginning this means just a few days of effort.

Gradually increase the requirements for the reward and increase the time it takes to earn the reward by one-day incre-

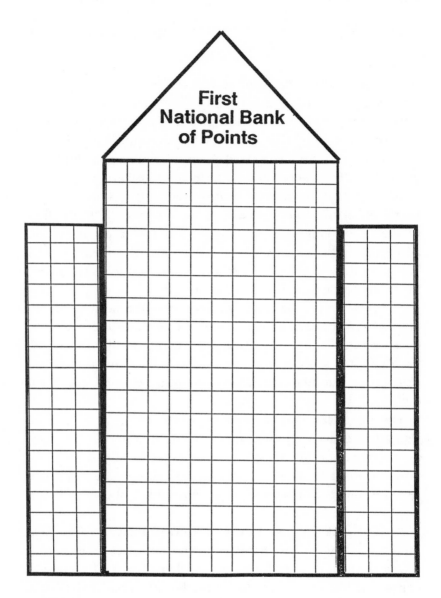

FIGURE 3.2
The First National Bank of Points

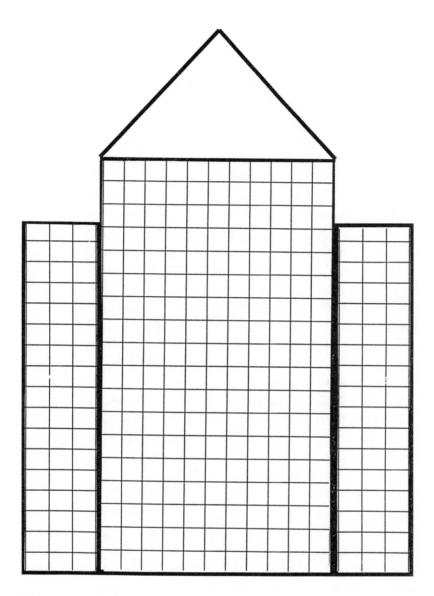

FIGURE 3.3
Jim's Bank of Points

ments. Over time, you will increase the requirements so that your child must show improvement to earn the same number of points. For the second dinner-time goal, Jim had to sit longer at the table to earn a point. This was more difficult for him, so it took a little longer for him to achieve the goal but he earned at least one point and a pull from the grab bag each step of the way.

In the game of Statue in Chapter 7, the child learns to sit still for increasing periods of time. The first time he follows directions, he may earn one point for sitting still for a few seconds. The next time he will earn one point for matching that record and two points for exceeding it. He would not earn points for lesser performance. As the child's control improves, the requirements for earning a reward naturally increase. Keep in mind, though, that if the cost of the rewards is so high that it seems impossible to earn the points to acquire them, the child will not be motivated to continue.

Slowly phase out daily rewards. When you see that the new behavior is fairly well established, slowly phase out the immediate rewards. Continue with the point system, surprising your child with an immediate reward every other work session, once in a while and then randomly.

Charts should be a visual record of your child's progress. The purpose of a chart is to illustrate your child's progress. The charts should be easy to read and simple to use. Throughout this book we have included charts that you may copy and use with your child. You may also order the charts and other materials discussed (see Appendix A).

By keeping in mind the following principles, you will be able to create effective charts for your own use.

• Chart one behavior (or cluster of behaviors) at a time. It is impossible to keep track of numerous behaviors simultaneously.

• Make a chart visually portray the developing behavior. Bar graphs are very helpful in this respect. A very simple bar graph shown in Figure 3.4 was used to depict Jim's increasing ability to sit at the dinner table. Each bar represents the number of minutes he sat at the table each day. Without stopping to read the actual minutes, it is apparent Jim is making progress. The charts and tables in this book are created with this principle in mind.

• Use the chart consistently. You must use the chart each time you work on the new behavior. Otherwise its effectiveness will be lost. That is another reason why the chart should be simple to use and maintain.

Use a variety of rewards. Rewards act as reinforcers for desirable behaviors. Anything that increases your child's motivation to try again or continue a behavior is a reward. It can be a

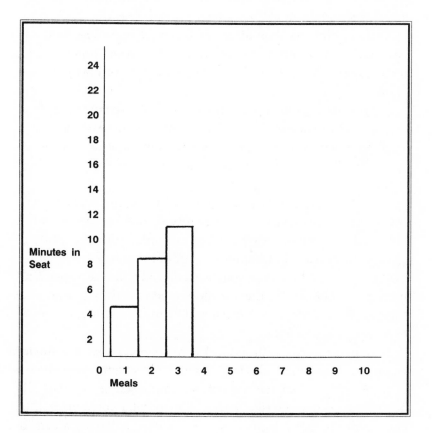

FIGURE 3.4
Jim's Bar Graph

privilege, a trinket, an activity or a material object. Any reward that is repeatedly employed will lose its appeal, so it is to your advantage to vary them.

To create a menu of items or activities from which your child can choose his reward, ask him about his preferences. You may copy the reinforcer survey in Figure 3.5 or create one of your own. Remembering the principles that have been discussed, it is then up to you to place a "price" on each reward. The rewards should be priced so that your child can easily earn some items within a brief period of time while others take longer.

Don't forget the praise. Always pair your specific praise with the points that you award. It makes both the praise and the points more meaningful. Ultimately your child will be working for your recognition and his own intrinsic pleasure.

Award points as soon after the behavior occurs as humanly possible. To be effective, points should be earned immediately. Instructions are given within each chapter about how to award points.

Keep your promises. Give the reward or exchange points at the time you promise. Avoid IOUs. You must deliver the goods. To a child, delay is a promise unkept. Points should be awarded immediately, and you should maintain a regular exchange schedule.

To make your point system most effective, insist on the rule that your child must spend all points earned toward a goal at the time the goal is reached. For example, with the game of Statue introduced in Chapter 7, your child will learn to sit for five minutes. When that goal is achieved, he must spend all points. Your child will then be motivated to earn new points for the next goal. This same rule should be in effect when you move to a new problem area.

Replace rewards with natural consequences once a behavior is very well established. Once a behavior is well established it is time to phase out the rewards by emphasizing the naturally occurring positive consequences of good behavior. This will be easy to do. In our system, rewards are used only as a means of establishing a new behavior. Once a goal is met, you will move on to a new behavior and another area of work. The well-established behavior should be reinforced by your continuing recognition, praise, natural consequences and, for good measure, an occasional surprise.

Natural consequences are the logical outcomes that follow a behavior. This type of reinforcement is totally in your control

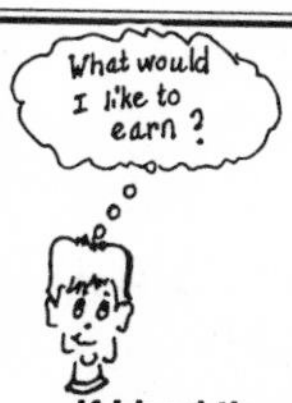

MY SUPER SURVEY

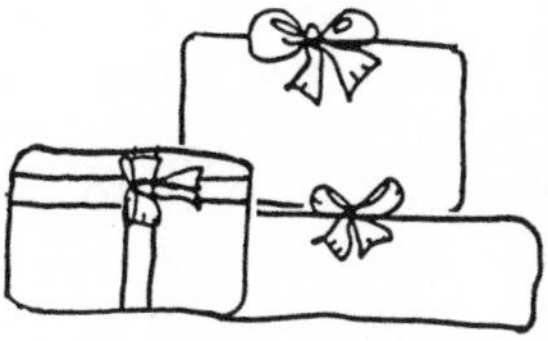

If I had three wishes , I'd wish...

____

And I'd wish...

____

My third wish would be...

____

Something I'd like to collect is ...

____

In my free time, three things I like to do are...

____

If I had 15 minutes with Dad, I'd like to

____

If I had more time with Dad it would be fun to ...

____

If I had fifteen minutes with Mom, I'd like to ...

____

If I had more time with Mom, I'd love to ...

____

Something I'd like to save my money for is ...

____

FIGURE 3.5
A Reinforcer Survey

and given as recognition for appropriate behavior. It is the natural payoff for performing well. When your child learns to sit at the dinner table and follow the rules of the table, one possible natural positive consequence is for the child to be allowed to go to a restaurant that was previously off-limits. When a child gets dressed quickly in the morning, this naturally leads to extra free time before the car pool comes. Learning how to complete five math problems in five minutes rather than forty-seven minutes might lead to extra television time.

■ *Negative Consequences*

It would be nice to think that your child or any child will respond so well to positive consequences that you will not need to apply any negative consequences. Unfortunately, that is rarely the way it works, especially for the child with ADHD characteristics. Although an emphasis on recognizing and building positive behavior must come first, sometimes other techniques are needed in order to motivate your child to change. In fact, as compared to other children, ADHD youngsters definitely appear to need more positive *and* negative consequences to change their behavior.

Sometimes the simplest and most effective way to change a child's behavior is to ignore it. Many of the most irritating behaviors of children are attention-seeking behaviors. Throwing a tantrum, whining and interrupting are often attention-seeking behaviors that can be effectively eliminated through systematic ignoring.

When you ignore a behavior, you must totally ignore all aspects of the behavior. From a quick glance to a direct response, you must remove all attention from the behavior. A slight look or a frown is frequently all it takes to prompt the negative behavior. You must not react to the unwanted behavior in any way. Look away, pretend you are busy, leave the room. If you cannot leave, then move to another area.

As soon as your child begins to act positively, or even neutrally, attend to him again. By systematically ignoring inappropriate behaviors and positively attending to the appropriate behaviors of your child, you focus a spotlight filled with your attention on appropriate behavior while directing the light away from undesirable behavior.

Often when attention is first removed, the old inappropriate behavior increases. If you think about it, the persistence makes sense. Throwing a tantrum always worked before—why not now? Your child will do his best to get the attention he is used to receiving.

Never choose to ignore a behavior unless you can stick with the decision. Once your child learns there will be no response, the behavior will decrease and finally stop, but if you give in, the tantrum or other attention-getting behavior will become more firmly entrenched.

There are times when it is necessary and appropriate to use negative consequences. The most effective negative consequences are those that are used sparingly, follow the undesired behavior immediately and are applied consistently. As a rule we do not recommend the use of physical punishment. It places you in the awkward position of modeling an undesirable behavior (hitting); nor is it the most productive technique at your disposal. Two negative consequences you can use more effectively are time-out and overcorrection.

Time-out is a technique that has been around for a very long time. Grandma had her corner long before the term time-out was coined. Time-out means time-out from positive reinforcement. It works best when your child has been reinforced through praise and rewards for appropriate behavior.

To use time-out, identify a location where your child is safe, bored, but feels that he is missing out on the action, and keep these principles in mind:

• Generally, time-out should be set according to the number of minutes in the child's age. For an eight-year-old that would mean eight minutes, for a three-year-old, three minutes. Long periods of time in a corner or the child's room are nonproductive. A short time-out period emphasizes the error of the child's ways but quickly gives him a chance to act appropriately.

Set a timer for the proper number of minutes, informing the child that if he is sitting quietly when the bell rings, he will be free to rejoin the activity.

• Add minutes for resistance. We are continually asked what to do if a child leaves the time-out chair. The answer is very simple with regard to a young child. Stand behind the child holding him in place. Matter-of-factly state that when he is calm and the bell sounds, he will be able to leave the seat. Avoid additional conversation.

For an older child, add one minute to the time-out period for each instance of resistance, not exceeding four extra minutes. If your child continues to resist, it is better to take away a privilege than struggle with a child you cannot forcibly keep in time-out.

• Ignore any outbursts from the child. Do not enter into discussions or lectures during or after time-out. This only gives the child attention at the wrong time and can prompt further outbursts. Again remove your attention totally until your child is out of time-out and beginning to act appropriately.

Overcorrection is another powerful technique to end persistent negative behaviors. Combined with what Dr. Nathan Azrin describes as positive practice, these techniques have the added advantage of teaching appropriate behavior. You will find them extremely effective alternatives to yelling and nagging.

• Undo the damage and teach a new response. From the child's point of view, you are asking him to "undo" the damage and "fix it." Of course, learning to consistently replace the undesirable behavior with a more positive one requires some practice of the new behavior. If your child impulsively pulls out toy after toy, leaving each one on the floor, use overcorrection to undo the behavior and teach him the new one. In this case the child is asked to put each toy in its proper place. Take the attitude that he obviously has not received enough practice in this skill.

• Overpractice the new behavior. After undoing a behavior, the child should then repeatedly practice more of the new behavior. After picking up the toys that were out of place originally, the youngster should join you in searching the house for other out-of-place items to put away. As another example, if a child runs into the street, he should return to the side, then overpractice the correct way to cross a street ten times.

• Supervise the practice session. If your child resists practicing, manually guide him through the correct actions. If he will not pick up the toys, hold his hands and guide them robot fashion through the task. Keep calm, ignoring any complaints or outbursts, but do remind your child that any time he needs more practice you will gladly oblige. With this power-packed technique, children learn that it is easier to do a task correctly the first time than to "practice."

Each of the techniques we have discussed in this chapter is used throughout this book. By knowing effective ways to promote the behaviors you seek to build, you will have the confidence to work with your child. There are many things you need to do, but the first step will be to gain your child's support. He needs to understand the goals you will seek together.

4

∎

How
to Explain
ADHD
to Your
Child

*F*or every parent
with a youngster who has been diagnosed as **ADHD**, one of the most difficult tasks is explaining **ADHD** to the child. Most parents fear saying the wrong thing, which could leave their child with the notion that he is defective or incapable of controlling his behavior. Others fear their explanation will frighten the child, becoming an excuse for misbehavior or a self-fulfilling prophecy.

To avoid anticipated pitfalls, some parents dodge the dilemma altogether. Others cloud the issue with yarns about little vitamin-like pills that must be taken twice a day to make a child big and strong. Avoidance seems an easy answer in the short run. But such shortcuts eventually hit roadblocks—for example, when a youngster continues to experience problems in school and elsewhere.

Consider six-year-old Jonathan. He knew something was wrong with him. His name was always on the board, he was the last one chosen for teams and no one ever invited him to play anymore. It was hard for him to finish his work at school so he frequently missed recess. Board work was the worst. He tried, but he couldn't keep his mind on his work. Frustrated and bewildered, he felt his self-confidence plummet.

You should explain ADHD to your child. You should tell him you realize it is difficult for him to sit still, stifle interruptions, keep his mind on a job or control his impulses. Otherwise, your child may conclude he is dumb or bad, as Jonathan did. Absent discussion, you and your child remain on opposite sides of the struggle. Inevitably, a child needs to understand ADHD.

There is no one time or right way to tell your youngster about ADHD, but there are some guidelines about which we feel quite strongly. Our years of experience working with children and their families have taught us several principles about discussing serious matters with children.

Keep it simple and honest.
Motivate your child to cope.
Validate your child's understanding.

Let's look at each of these three points to see how you can make them work for your family.

1. Keep it simple and honest. Whatever explanation you elect to use, your interpretation should adhere to the facts about ADHD. Talk to your child at his level of understanding. Consider his personality and tolerance for information. Does he prefer a lot of details or just a few brief facts? Is she easily frightened by discussions that relate to body function? Since there are many ways to approach the task, it is unlikely any truthful explanation will be "wrong." A couple of examples will make this point.

Cal was seven. He had never sat at the table for an entire meal. Many evenings, however, both parents repeatedly tried to get Cal to sit in his chair. Invariably, completely worn down, they would finally allow him to leave as everyone else continued eating the main course. After one of these unpleasant dinners, Dad found Cal later that night playing with his collection of little cars. He suggested they have a little talk. "Cal, you know it's very difficult for you to sit at the table, isn't it? I bet it feels like we're always fussing at you. But, son, I want to have dinner with you; I want to hear about your day. Mom and I realize you do have more trouble sitting still. It's also harder for you to go to sleep at night. We want to help you learn to sit a little longer at the table so we can get to dessert together...."

Jamie had a different sort of problem. Jamie is a bright ten-year-old who came home crying because his classmates called him hyper and teased him about taking hyper pills. Rather than avoiding the facts one more time, Jamie's mom decided to give an explanation a try. On this occasion, his mother asked Jamie what he thought hyper meant. Jamie answered, "Crazy wild." This gave her the opening she needed. Immediately his mom began correcting his misinformation. First, she assured Jamie he was neither crazy nor wild. "In fact," she said, "you are a very bright boy. But sometimes it takes you longer to do your work, not because you don't know the right answers, but because it's difficult for you to keep your mind on your work."

Both Cal's dad and Jamie's mom used simple words to describe what they noticed about their child's behavior and to acknowledge that sitting still and focusing attention were difficult for these youngsters. The descriptions were simple and honest because they meshed with the facts as everyone knew them.

2. Your explanation should motivate your child to cope. Your explanation should provide a stepping-off point for your family to work together to manage the effects of ADHD. Besides providing a basic definition, you are trying to interpret ADHD so that your child is motivated to cope with and even overcome the symptoms. The rest of Jamie's story makes this point well.

Agreeing that he found it hard to concentrate on his work, Jamie exclaimed, "But that doesn't explain why they call me hyper!" Continuing, his mother explained that hyper was an abbreviation for a word he had heard before, hyperactive, which means always moving and unable to sit still for long.

Jamie instantly recognized that this did not describe him at all. "Other kids at school take medication for hyperactivity, but not me," he told her.

Jamie's mom then asked him what he thought his problems were. With only a brief hesitation, Jamie said that his real problems were daydreaming and being interested in all the stuff going on around him so that his teacher was always annoyed with him for not completing his work. As a result he would get frustrated and sometimes angry if his classmates teased him about how slow he was. His mom was actually a little surprised by her son's astute understanding of his problems. She confirmed his conclusions that his real problems related to concentration and being overly sensitive to the comments of peers.

3. Validate your child's understanding of ADHD. With our previous suggestions in mind, Jamie's mother took the discussion one step further. She did not ask him what he understood about ADHD, but questioned what kinds of things were difficult for him. She asked him about other things he did outside the classroom about which the kids might tease him. With a little prodding, she turned Jamie's focus to the playground: Why are you often picked near the last for teams? He offered the fact that it was hard for him to keep his mind, much less his eyes, on the ball. She told him how that too fit the pattern of ADHD. Jamie's mom asked him what he could do if his classmates needled him again. Together they came up with some retorts he could use.

During these conversations, Jamie gained some accurate information he could apply in several ways. He learned there were different forms of ADHD and that he could manage his problems better. Armed with a few comebacks, Jamie was ready the next time when a peer called him "hyper." "I am not hyperactive, I just have a distractibility problem and the pills help me concentrate better!" A few days later he told his mom he was really surprised that the other students said very little. Whether they were stunned by his sudden confidence or simply not prepared to pursue the issue further, they left him alone for a little while.

As Jamie repeated this explanation to other students and found them more accepting, he gradually shared other bits of information with his friends. "I can't talk or even look up when you say something to me in class. I have to stay on track. I will talk to you later on at the playground." In a curious way this explanation became less an excuse for Jamie and more of an inspiration. His classmates learned not to bother him in class, and he was motivated to pull himself away from the distractions that remained.

There are many explanations you can use with your youngster. Just remember to keep them simple and be honest. Look for ways not only to explain ADHD but to provide a rationale that helps your child cope with the problems associated with it. In the following sections we will furnish some approaches that have worked for other parents. Among them you may find an explanation that you can tailor to your child.

• The younger the child, the more elementary the explanation needs to be. Children do not want a lot of extraneous information. They prefer to know only what they need to know to understand the situation. Do not feel pressured to tell your child everything you know about ADHD. He cannot digest all of the details in one setting. Over the years you will have many opportunities to add to his store of information.

• As a general rule, avoid diagnostic labels. More important than a name are some simple facts that make sense to your child. It is helpful to introduce the vocabulary that explains the symptoms: attention, distractibility, impulsiveness, etc.

• Make the explanation one that helps your child relate to the symptoms he has. Most youngsters love imaginative stories told with a little show-biz razzmatazz. We often use animal characterizations and analogies to get our point across. Few six-year-olds have observed animals in the jungle, but they instantly relate to the concept of a "tiger in their tank" to demonstrate the rambunctiousness they feel. To Cal, the six-year-old who could not sit at the table long enough to complete his meal, his dad suggested there was a tiger in his tank they needed to tame together. Pleased with this notion, Cal exclaimed, "Yeah, I'll get him to be still. I'll stand on his tail!" Rather than feeling guilty about his restlessness, Cal was motivated to work with his dad toward a reasonable goal.

With a child who is particularly interested in mechanical objects, an example of a runaway freight train or a supercharged motor that only he can bring under control might work equally well as the tiger. The parent of a five-year-old who was mesmerized by trains first read her child the story of *The Little Engine Who Could* by Piper Watty. Then she suggested that sometimes her young son became so wound up, he was like a runaway train barreling out of control around the house. Perhaps, she suggested, like the Little Engine, they too could put their heads together and work on self-control. "I think I can" became the family motto.

From robots to volcanoes to superheroes with extraordinary powers, any topic that focuses on channeling energy suggests a good working explanation. It all depends on the child's age and interests and what you can seize upon to hold his attention.

The same approach will work to explain concentration and impulse control to the young child. Our favorite description is the deer in the forest who hears a noise in the woods. From storybooks and movies, Jonathan, the child who felt so bad about his ability to complete his work, knew that a deer looks toward a sound, freezing in place until it discovers whether the source is friend or foe. Since Jonathan had seen the Walt Disney film *Bambi,* he knew that the little rabbit was rather impulsive and frequently failed to wait long enough to identify the source of a sound so he didn't get into trouble. Using Jonathan's comments, his mom explained, "You are very good at hearing sounds, but sometimes you don't know which ones are important to listen to, so you listen for everything. If your teacher gives you directions, you hear them, but when she talks to another group of children you listen to those instructions, then to the children talking behind you, to a yell in the hall and to a truck going down the street outside the school." Using your child's comments, you can easily adapt your characterizations to explain the concepts of selective attention, knowing what to pay attention to, and sustaining attention, which is maintaining attention long enough to complete a task.

Jonathan's mother suggested, "I'd like to help you work on learning what to listen to and what to ignore so you can finish your work."

▪ Relate your explanation to your child's typical symptoms. Once you have developed a working concept, the next step is to use illustrations from your child's life to generalize the explanation. For instance, perhaps you have talked about how impetuous the little rabbit in *Bambi* is to explain the notion of impulsivity. You have been working on teaching your child how to cross the street. He knows he must stop, look both ways and wait long enough to be sure it is safe to cross. What would happen if the ball ran into the street and he darted after it without pausing? Is he as aware that pausing and waiting to gather the necessary information is important in less dangerous situations also? Would it also be true for attending to parents' instructions long enough to find out what the family is going to do next or listening to the teacher's directions to find out how to do an assignment the right way? With each of these examples the little rabbit may be a helpful example to illuminate the concept so your child recognizes the importance of trying to attend better.

▪ Provide as much information as the older child wants. By third grade most ADHD children are experiencing significant strains, no matter how well they are coping. The child needs to grasp the nature of his problems but usually also seeks some knowledge about why he is having these particular difficulties. Now it is appropriate to begin to reveal how attentional processes work, since this is the source of much of his difficulty.

Initiate a discussion of individual differences. Upper elementary school students are aware of who is good at what. If you ask your child who is the best reader in his class, who is good at math, who is considerate of other people's feelings, who runs the fastest, he can tell you. With little difficulty your child will accept the idea that some children are good at particular skills while other youngsters have different talents. This basic understanding of individual differences also applies to attentional abilities.

Extend the discussion to yourself. Children are fascinated with the idea that one of their parents is also better at concentrating than the other. Perhaps Mom can read a novel while the television squawks in the background and the family members are talking, but maybe that would not work at all for Dad. He must enter his study and close the door when he wants to concentrate. The concept of filters provides an uncomplicated but satisfying reason for this difference. Mom simply has better filters in her mind; she can block the extraneous noise that comes her way to continue reading. On the other hand, Dad's filters may not be as strong. That is not his fault; it happens to be the way he is, but it does put more of a strain on him so he is not able to attend as long without getting tired. If other family members illustrate your point more effectively, use them instead.

Ultimately the ADHD child knows that we are talking about him and that the reasons he has difficulty concentrating are similar. The illustration in Figure 4.1 will help you describe how the brain acts like a computer. Like the computer it receives input; but, unlike a computer, the brain is constantly bombarded with information assembled through many different means, including sight, hearing, smell, taste and touch. Simultaneously, there are messages coming to the brain from within the body, including feelings of fullness or hunger, hot or cold, thirst, fatigue or energy, and comfort or pain. Finally there is information from inside the brain—old memories, worries or preoccupation with things that are happening today, and even fears and hopes about future events—that competes for attention. This is quite a lot of input for any brain to sort out and control. Constructively explain that some brains handle this fairly well, but for some people the thoughts occur so rapidly, the impulses are so bold, and the feelings so sensitive that they overwhelm the filters of the control center.

The control center does not intend all the extraneous stuff to get through, but sometimes this occurs nonetheless. Once so much excess information enters, the control center gets con-

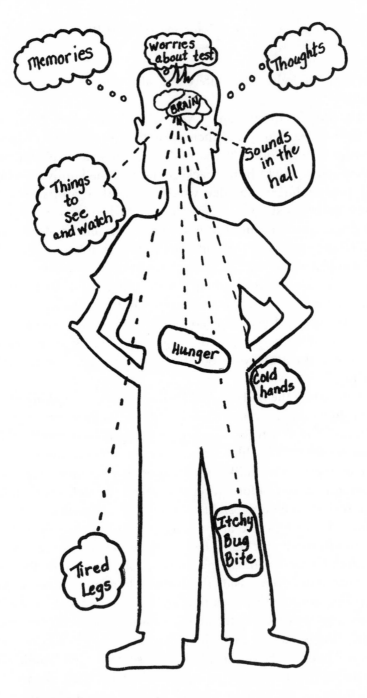

FIGURE 4.1
The Brain as Control Center

fused and does not know what to focus on any longer. Every stimulus starts jockeying for recognition. First the control center recognizes the hunger in the stomach, the pants that do not feel right, and then a thought about what is for dinner. Similar to a TV set that is continually switching channels, a person with this problem has a hard time getting a sense of what's going on or what is relevant. In the child's case, he becomes so busy reacting to stimuli that he may be attending to the wrong things when pertinent directions are given and may not recognize which information is important at the moment. As he struggles to sort out the incoming information, his impulses compete for recognition also. Sometimes they are so strong that they override or completely avoid the censoring mechanism that is supposed to prevent ideas from crystallizing before they escape into words or actions.

A similar interpretation can be employed to explain why many ADHD children are perpetual-motion machines. The child's body is in constant motion because the impulses are radiating without any deterrence from the control center. With nothing to impede his impulses, a child can easily be out of his seat, by the window, touching a pencil, and running his hands over the wallpaper without thinking twice about it.

As we suggested in the case of the younger child, explanations must be presented in a manner that motivates a child to cope and strive to overcome the problems. Yes, he has more trouble filtering out stimuli, but now that he's aware of this difficulty, he can offer some assistance to his control center. In Chapters 7 through 13 you will learn how to help him do just that.

▪ With teenagers, de-emphasize the differences. Explaining anything to a teenager in a way that will not turn him off is the biggest challenge of all. Double that for the ADHD teen. First, you must remember that adolescents cannot tolerate anything that makes them the least bit different—hair, clothes, friends. A pimple is as big a problem as a bad test grade. Wearing glasses or anything else that sets them apart is a major disaster. Second, teenagers resist any solution to a problem suggested by a parent. As a rule, just getting on the same wavelength as your adolescent is a major accomplishment.

With this in mind, how then do you explain ADHD in a manner that engenders understanding and cooperation? If you have been dealing with this issue for a while, your explanations have evolved through the years. If you have avoided the topic or have just discovered the problem, you may have to pursue this goal slightly more gently.

- Respect the adolescent. Talk to your adolescent one on one, as you would to another adult. Honesty is crucial, so do not attempt to hide anything. Acknowledge there is a problem, then pinpoint its characteristics. "You have trouble paying attention long enough to complete your homework in a single sitting. It is not just because the work is boring; you have a naturally short attention span, so you will have to work around it. You are easily distracted by things going on around you; in the classroom this makes it hard for you to concentrate on what a teacher is saying. Your mind tends to wander off the subject. Sometimes, although you do not mean to, your impulsiveness gets you into difficult situations."

- Provide resources to corroborate and expand the information. Most teenagers want to know why this is happening to them. Sometimes it is best to let them hear a formal explanation from an unrelated person whom the child knows and respects. It might be his physician or therapist. Other teens may prefer to read about the problem. You might start with this book, or select a few resources from Appendix B. If there is a local support group for children with ADHD, your son or daughter may find it helpful to discuss these issues and exchange information in the group. Occasionally parents are able to link their adolescent with an older college student who has successfully coped with these problems, who then becomes a model for the younger child. One fourteen-year-old who was extremely reluctant to discuss any aspect of ADHD came away from a meeting with a senior football star who also happened to have attentional problems with a new view of the situation. Probably no amount of information from a parent or professional could have changed this youngster's attitude as quickly.

- Join with your teenager in developing solutions to old problems. Once you have broken through the barrier to talking about ADHD, your teen will be more receptive to information. The computer-control example is still valid and a good starting point for discussion. Most teenagers want access only to the information they need today. Long before you explained ADHD, they knew they had difficulties. If you are lucky, they may accept help now. When you begin to discuss the attentional problems that plague your child, you may be met by a sigh of relief. This means you are on the right track. If your son finds it impossible to listen to lecture classes and is always getting in trouble for not listening, then knowing this may provide an impetus to give it a new try. Being able to say to himself and maybe even to a friend or two that he is having trouble concentrating in history class and needs to sit in the front is a big step. Adolescents need a strong rationale to be brave enough to verbalize the difficulty. Sometimes the explanation and label provide it.

After identifying your teen's particular set of problems, let him see this book. Point out the chapters that are relevant. Discuss how you might work on each aspect of the problem in a new way, together.

▪ Validate your adolescent's feelings and fears. Remember how you felt when your physician or psychologist told you your child was ADHD. No matter how sophisticated we get, when we hear a diagnosis about our child, it is emotionally draining. It takes time to comprehend the significance of the information and sometimes to accept its meaning. Your adolescent is in the same position. He will have some questions now and more later. Sometimes those questions will turn into denial. Other times his fear will affect his outlook. The emotions will jumble, and you will not be able to predict his response. Stick with it. Be there for him, and eventually you will reach some understanding that allows you both to cope more effectively with ADHD.

5
■

Gaining
Acceptance
and Support
from Siblings,
Other Relatives,
Friends, Teachers
and Others

*I*f your child has to wear eyeglasses, you would be sure to mention it to his teacher so that she can seat him in a position where he can clearly view the blackboard. And certainly, she would be glad you shared the information. Or if your child has a hearing problem, you would no doubt inform her of this so she could keep this in mind when working with your child.

So why are you reluctant to tell others that your youngster has difficulty sitting still or finds it hard to concentrate? Many parents readily share this information, while others become almost obsessed with the idea that the fewer individuals who know about it, the better. Almost every parent of an ADHD child worries about whom to tell and how much.

Ironically, though, while most ADHD children's behaviors are far from hidden, many parents elect to hide the facts. Unfortunately, the result of secrecy is innuendo. When others are not informed they are likely to speculate instead: "Why don't his parents teach him how to behave? His parents are way too easy. That child has a real problem." As a result, a lot of negative attention is heaped on the child as people "discuss" his problem.

How others will react is clearly one of the main concerns most parents of ADHD children have. What will Aunt Ida think? Will Uncle Henry worry his nephew is unstable? Will our next-door neighbor let our children continue to play together? How will our child be labeled? And finally, if I share this information, will it do any good?

When you are parenting an ADHD child twenty-four hours a day, it takes an enormous amount of energy to deal with the outside world. In our experience, parents have been pleasantly surprised with the support they receive when they take the time to explain the nature of their child's problem and their ways of dealing with it. Each time you share your situation with another person who comes in contact with your child, you are making them part of the plan, giving them an opportunity to support your child and stand in his corner.

The ADHD child does not live in a vacuum, and neither do you. His behavior spills over, affecting those near and dear as well as those less involved. Unless they understand why he acts the ways he does, they are likely to misjudge him and even you.

When a child overhears others calling him hyper, a troublemaker, or worse, the labels contribute to a negative self-image that is not easily shaken. Some of this is unavoidable. But by sharing information with people significantly involved in his life, you increase the chances that your child will be supported rather than ridiculed. You are stacking the odds in your child's favor.

How you explain ADHD as it relates to your child is certainly a delicate issue—more so with some people than with others. Remember, though, you are in control of the information flow. You can decide who needs to know, when and how much.

■ *The Role You and Your Spouse Play*

We hope that you and your spouse are both reading this book. Any support your child gains from others is secondary to the backing he receives from his immediate family. Sharing the responsibility for educating and raising an ADHD child lightens the load on everyone in the family. Whether you live with your child's other parent or not, if you have a common understanding of ADHD and how it affects your child, you have a better chance to help him. If you have not discussed these issues, don't wait any longer. Perhaps Dad exhibited many of these behaviors as a child; maybe Mom cannot accept the fact that her child has a problem. Whatever is on your mind, bring it out in the open.

Once you are in agreement, it will be easier for you to share the task of talking to others. As you decide to whom you are going to talk, remember that your main goal is to gain the individual's support. To do that, keep your explanations factual and simple. Most important, provide suggestions for how that person can help.

■ *Telling Siblings*

Although ADHD is very hard on your child and you, it is also tough on your child's siblings. Although they themselves do not have the deficit, frequently they bear the brunt of the situation. Ten-year-old Roger resented the fact that his eight-year-old brother Seth got all the attention. It did not matter that most of it was negative. Seth was always center stage. It always seemed to Roger that special allowances were made for his brother: "They're always changing the rules for him, but when it comes to me, I'm supposed to know better."

It is hard enough to be anybody's sibling, but even more difficult when you are the sister or brother of an ADHD child. Every situation is complicated by something the ADHD child does or does not do. Either his impulsiveness disrupts the activity or he is never ready to get started. Conversations at the dinner table are interrupted, toys are broken, and every game ends with an argument.

The most common and telling complaint of the sibling is that he is embarrassed. Roger explained this well. "Every time we go somewhere, Seth is always doing something that people stare at. At the grocery store, he knocks over displays or yells he wants candy. At school he's in trouble, in the car pool he fights over where to sit. He even hits my mom when she tells him to stop. If I did that I'd lose television for a year!"

Observations like these are not unusual. Siblings of ADHD kids feel the stress, the frustrations and the additional obstacles that complicate the routine for the family. Do not underestimate the effects. How you approach your ADHD child's brothers and sisters can make a difference in gaining their understanding and support. Explanations can be more complicated when the ADHD child is older than the sibling. You must wait until the younger sibling is not only old enough to understand the disorder but also able to use the information wisely.

• Explain. Using the relevant information in Chapter 4, explain ADHD to your child's siblings. Although you may add to the discussion, be sure to include the account you gave to the ADHD child himself.

• Identify the characteristics of ADHD and explain how they influence the ADHD child's behavior. The notion that everyone has both strengths and weaknesses is very important. Alyce's mother was very wise when she began her conversation with an older brother: "You are able to do addition problems very quickly and you almost always come inside when I call you. But you know sometimes when you do your homework, your mind starts to wander, doesn't it? Alyce's mind wanders too, but it's harder for her to concentrate, so she gets off course more often —kind of like a kite that sails wherever the wind takes it. Of course if you tug on the string, the kite comes back. That's what happens to Alyce when she's getting dressed or when she forgets what she's doing when you're playing a game."

• Encourage the siblings to express feelings. Siblings should have the opportunity to vent how they feel. In some families pent-up anger fuels squabbles and bickering, jealousy and resentment. Expressing those negative feelings can diffuse the situation, making room for new experiences.

• Give attention regularly. ADHD children take a lot of time. Since siblings seem to require less maintenance and are more reliable, they may unintentionally get short-changed. Each child needs time alone with you. Arrange special activities with each child individually so your attention does not have to be divided.

If you are working with your ADHD child on a particular aspect of his behavior, avoid working on the same behavior with a sibling. It is fine, though, to encourage a sibling to work on another aspect of his own behavior that could use a little improvement. Although the siblings will both be earning points, there should be little competition between them.

• Share new solutions. Certainly you do not think other families have no problems. Not all conflicts between siblings are the result of one child being ADHD. When there is a consistent problem, such as fighting over the television or questions related to ownership, define the problem and devise a plan together to change the situation.

• Provide separate opportunities for each child. Children need their own space, friends and activities. Try to treat each child as an individual, selecting extracurricular programs, activities and playmates with that in mind.

■ *Telling the Grandparents*

Grandparents are very special people. Along with that loving relationship automatically comes affection, interest and advice, which can yield support for your child and for you. Although we tend to forget, grandparents were parents once, and they handled the trials and tribulations of raising kids. Regardless of the fact that they now view their grandchildren as their perfect legacy to the world, they can learn to view these young links to immortality with objectivity.

There are two main reasons grandparents may have difficulty accepting this information. First, when they were raising you, ADHD was not a familiar term. Second, because they may not see your children from the same point of view, they may be unaware of some of the behaviors that distress you. Let's face it. When children go to Grandma's and Grandpa's to play, there are likely to be many fewer rules to follow—in some cases, none at all. Since they do not see your children every day, they may be unaware of the gyrations you have gone through and may assume that your parenting is lax.

Many initially unsupportive grandparents do an about-face when given time. They learn to bolster parental efforts and to follow through on their own.

If you had a difficult time accepting your child's problems, then you immediately understand the mixed feelings grandparents experience. What grandparents bring with them is unconditional love for their grandchild. If you give them the information they need, time to digest it, and suggestions of ways to help, you can continue to promote that very special relationship between children and grandparents.

• **Explain ADHD and offer educational materials.** Talking to grandparents at every step of the way is very helpful. Sharing your concerns is better than being defensive. If your family is staying with Grandma for the holidays, she will probably see many sides of your child's behavior. Telling her how you have been approaching the situation, sharing information you have been given and even attending a support group or lecture together may be very helpful. Provide some simple reading matter from this book or other selections you have found helpful.

• **Make time for Grandma and Grandpa.** If your child rarely sees the grandparents, then try to plan for those occasions with all the diligence of an army colonel. Try to keep the event low-key and casual, with as few rules as possible. A trip to the park or a movie is likely to be more fun than dinner at a fancy restaurant. If your child will be staying with the grandparents for any length of time, you must share the elements of the routine that work for you. "Listen, Dad, roughhousing with Roger before bedtime is not a good idea. And the days go better if he knows what to expect." If the grandparents elect not to use your suggestions this time, they probably will next time.

■ *Telling Other Family Members*

How much you tell aunts, uncles, cousins and other family members depends on how much your child must interact with them. If you see them only on Thanksgiving and the Fourth of July every other year, then you may say nothing at all. You will manage in the situation, and by the time the holiday comes around again, your child will have learned many skills.

If a relative is very close to your family, then you will want that person to understand your child. Since there is evidence that ADHD runs in families, you may have more to commiserate about than you ever suspected. Having family members on your side is good for you and your child.

■ *Telling Teachers*

A teacher is a person who spends many hours with your child every day, whose sole purpose is to help your child grow. Of course you must tell your child's teachers.

Teachers know children. They have viewed many kids of the same age in many situations. Your child's teacher will probably be aware of some outstanding behavior your child exhibits. Many parents worry they will predispose the teacher not to like the child if they reveal that their youngster has ADHD. On the other hand, if you are just beginning the diagnostic process, input from his teacher is crucial. Since you will be working with a professional during the diagnostic process, that person will help with the communication.

Although most teachers have been educated about ADHD, they are not familiar with your child or the ways you are working with him. After an initial conference, it may be appropriate to request a formal meeting involving all of the school staff who will be working with your child. A more detailed discussion of how to work with your child's school is provided in Chapter 16.

■ *The Immediate World*

Your child comes in contact with so many people every day. He does not need to be labeled for each one of them. While you must consider your child's special needs, do not avoid situations. Plan for them. As you work through this book, you will gain a variety of skills that will ready you and your child for the world away from home.

Depending on the situation, tell individuals who interact with your child what they need to know to have a positive experience with him. If your son is playing baseball, putting him in the outfield is likely to be disastrous. He would never pay attention long enough to be ready for a ball coming his way. Sharing this information with the coach allows him to do a better job choosing a position for your child. Similarly, informing the host parents at a sleep-over party that your child is likely to be up long after the other guests unwind would be appreciated. If you send a flashlight and a quiet toy along with your son, you will make the evening less stressful for everyone.

6
■

If,
When
and How
to Use
Medication

*U*ndoubtedly, one of the most difficult decisions you face as a parent of a child who is hyperactive or has attentional deficits is whether to use medication. Unlike an antibiotic taken for a few days to remedy an infection, the drugs prescribed to control ADHD require long-term courses of treatment.

The sensational media coverage on the use of Ritalin and other drugs to treat ADHD has done little to inform the public about the facts involved. Although many of the issues journalists have raised about the misuse of medication concern us, a great deal of misinformation about the medications has been presented as fact.

When we first began working with ADHD children more than

seventeen years ago, we believed we could help these young-sters through the use of behavioral and educational techniques alone. That was true for some kids, but for others medication was not only helpful but essential. It was virtually impossible for the latter group to sustain their attention without the proper type and dosage of medication. More important, on medication, the educational interventions and behavior therapy techniques that worked for others now worked much better with them. The difference between these children on medication and the same children off it was striking. When they were off medication, there was a marked deterioration in their schoolwork and other functioning. When they were on medication, their ability to control aspects of their behavior improved markedly and their attention and concentration also increased. Cautiously and re-luctantly we came to the conclusion that for these children, the appropriate use of the right medication was more than simply helpful—it made a real difference for that child.

This was not an easy discovery for us to accept. As we talked with colleagues, we were reassured to find that their observa-tions were the same. Over time, we felt more comfortable with these opinions as a number of carefully controlled scientific studies confirmed that a combination of behavioral therapy and medication was far superior to either treatment alone. We are convinced that although medication should *never* be the only thing you do to help an ADHD child, using medication should not be ruled out because of preconceived notions.

When parents ask us, "Can my child be helped without med-ication?" our answer is often "It depends." If your child's prob-lems are mild and only in specific areas, he may be able to learn to control his activity level, beat distractions, lengthen his at-tention span or become less impulsive by the methods de-scribed in this book. Others with learning problems will require these interventions plus special educational help. In smaller classroom settings with specialized teaching, some students who previously completed their schoolwork only with the help of medication may find they are able to do as well without medication. But—and this is a big but—many others need med-ication as well as every other kind of help available to tune into the situation long enough to do well and feel good about them-selves. It all depends on the child. If your child has moderate to severe **ADHD**, he will probably need a combination of both medication and other interventions in order to cope.

To put your child on medication you must feel that he will be safe from long-term harm and believe that the medication is necessary for his well-being. Because medicating a child is never the only possible treatment, you will want to understand why it has been recommended for your child before you proceed with medication. To make your decision, you probably will have to have many questions answered. In this chapter we shall answer the questions that have been posed to us most often by parents grappling with the decision of whether to try medica-tion. Then, for those of you who want to try medication for your child, under your doctor's supervision, of course, and for those of you whose child is already using a prescribed drug, we will discuss the best way to monitor its effectiveness, permitting you to feel safe.

If my child does go on medication,
what are the chances it will help him?

Not every child who is having attentional problems needs medication. Only those children who are diagnosed as **ADHD** after a carefully conducted assessment by trained professionals should be considered as candidates for medication.

Of those children who are properly diagnosed as **ADHD**, ap-proximately 75 percent show a positive response to medical intervention. Even among the children who do respond, the amount of improvement varies tremendously. Of the other 25 percent of nonresponders, most show only temporary improve-ment or no effect at all. A small percentage of children on med-ication become more hyperactive or inattentive or show other negative reactions to the drug. The reaction is easily noticed by both parents and teachers within a few days. Some children who have no response to the first drug prescribed, typically Ritalin, may show a positive response to another medication; others never do.

The only way to know how your child will respond to medication is to follow the guidelines that have been prescribed and try it.

Can I tell if my child is ADHD
by putting him on medication?

It is a mistake to assume that because a child responds to medication he must be ADHD. The fact that a child does *not* respond to medication says nothing about his condition. It certainly does not indicate that his problems are less real than those who do respond. A child may respond temporarily to medication, whether or not he or she really needs it. Our stand is clear—a child who has not been formally diagnosed ADHD should never be put on medication on the chance it can improve his performance.

Unfortunately much of the controversy surrounding the use of medication probably radiates from these misconceptions. There have been cases where children who have other medical or psychological problems were placed on medication without proper testing first. The resulting problems might have occurred anyway. Perhaps the medication intensified their symptoms. Although it is hard to know why they had difficulty, the medication was not helpful. As a result of negative public and media attention, many parents have become fearful and have developed preconceived notions about medication without having access to the facts or the opportunity to talk to the parents of children who have been greatly helped by medical interventions without experiencing any negative side effects.

How does the medication work?

Many parents feel guilty about having their child take medication because they mistakenly think they are tranquilizing him. The most commonly used medications for ADHD are actually stimulants, not tranquilizers. The idea that a very active, impulsive child should be put on a stimulant in order to slow him down may seem strange at first. For many years, researchers thought this paradoxical effect was simply another quirk of the disorder. Actually the contradictions are only on the surface. These medications stimulate parts of the brain that help the child concentrate more intensely and for longer periods of time. When a child's activity is more focused, he naturally becomes less active and as a result appears calmer.

The decrease in external movement because of medication does not mean he has been tranquilized. A similar effect is noticed when an ADHD child becomes locked into a constantly changing stimulus, such as television or a video game. In these activities, most ADHD youngsters seem oblivious to the outside world. This does not mean that they are tranquilized by the electronic medium, but that their attention is temporarily focused so that they seem mesmerized.

There are hazards involved in overmedication. With too high a dosage, a child may appear tranquilized, even lethargic, so that he is unable to attend to anything at all. Too much medication thus not only decreases activity level but also hurts attention.

Are there side effects?
Will they disappear?

Any medication can have side effects; while the person taking the drug may not experience any side effects, there is always some risk. If you look up almost any medication in a consumer or professional drug compendium, from aspirin to zinc, there is an unnerving catalog of possible side effects. Some pre-existing conditions may preclude the use of a particular drug because of possible side effects.

The medications used to treat ADHD, from methylphenidate (Ritalin) to pemoline (Cylert), also have potential side effects. Many of these are temporary as the child's body adjusts to the medication. Some children may never experience these extraneous symptoms, while others will continue as long as the child is taking the medication.

The most common side effect of the kinds of stimulants used to treat ADHD involve appetite suppression. Again, many children never experience this or experience it only mildly, and it disappears after a few days or weeks. For a child with pounds to spare, this may be less of a concern, but a finicky eater who is already slim has little excess weight. To circumvent such a problem, the medication must be timed so it interferes with meals as little as possible. Families find a variety of solutions. Some parents get their child up a little early and serve him breakfast before giving him the pill. Others plan extra snacks and food supplements at times during the day when the effects of the medication are waning. If this is your child's problem, your overriding concern is whether the appetite suppression will affect his growth. You will need the help of your family doctor or pediatrician to check your child's growth, both weight and height, periodically, to make sure he is following the same growth pattern he did before starting medication.

Several years ago, there was a lot of discussion about the long-term effects of stimulant medication on the child's growth pattern. Children were given drug holidays on weekends and summer vacations in order to catch up. Now that more research data have been accumulated and youngsters who have been taking the medication for years have been closely monitored, there is much less concern about this factor. No significant differences in growth curves on and off medication were found in most youngsters when they have been followed through adolescence. As long as a child consumes the appropriate amount of nourishment during the day, in the long run his growth will continue on course no matter how erratic his eating habits may seem to be to worried parents.

A second side effect that sometimes occurs is insomnia. Depending on when a child takes his last dose of medication, a rebound effect may occur because the medication is wearing off. As a result the child becomes so restless that he is unable to fall asleep. You are already aware that many ADHD youngsters need less sleep than their peers and many resist bedtime anyway, so all bedtime problems cannot be blamed on the medication. If taking medication contributes to sleep problems, then the medication can be timed in such a way as to overcome this effect.

Some of the medications are available in short-acting and time-released forms. Taking the short-acting medications early enough for the effects to wear off usually works for most children. As an alternative, some physicians avoid any rebound by prescribing a smaller dose of medication, closer to bedtime, which permits the child to control his impulses enough to settle down and get to sleep. At times physicians will prescribe additional medications that counteract the effects of the stimulant.

There are a number of less frequently reported side effects, including headaches, stomachaches, dizziness and other physical symptoms. Emotional symptoms like moodiness, irritability and crying spells have also been reported. While some of these are real side effects, many could have been going on before the child ever took any medication. In a recent survey of such side effects, Dr. Russell Barkley reported in the *Clinical Child Psychology Newsletter* of the American Psychological Association that the ADHD children in his sample had the same number of reported symptoms, which might also be labeled as side effects, before and after they went on medication.

One side effect of stimulant medications may not be temporary. Many young children go through periods in their life when they exhibit some form of nervous tic. From eye blinking and facial twitches to throat clearing or shoulder jerking, these tics are usually annoying, especially to bystanders, but relatively harmless. Most of these tics are transient, disappearing after a few weeks or months, never to reappear. Others come and go intermittently. Some are replaced by other tics. Often tics occur in children who are high-strung or nervous. Occasionally these tics signal a much more serious condition known as Gilles de la Tourette's syndrome. If a person has Tourette's syndrome, the tics become more intense and lasting, often accompanied by uncontrollable language. If a child already displays any of these patterns, there is a slight chance that stimulant medication can worsen the condition. These symptoms often remain after the medication is discontinued. It is essential that a child who shows signs of tics be carefully evaluated by an expert before ever taking any medication.

Any child taking a prescribed medication should be closely monitored by his regular doctor, regardless of whether there are any apparent side effects. These are still stimulant medications that increase certain body processes. Your doctor will probably want to check vital signs regularly or do periodic blood work. A child can develop other conditions that preclude taking certain medications.

Will my child become dependent on medication
and abuse drugs as a result?

Naturally you worry about this, but the good news is that no research has found a clear relationship between taking medication for ADHD earlier in life and a propensity to become an abuser of alcohol or drugs later on. In fact, some youngsters adopt stands of staunch opposition to any drugs.

Somewhere around the time they hit adolescence a number of kids who had cooperated previously now become resistant to taking their medication. In the meantime, more than a few little pills end up fertilizing houseplants and magnolias. Unaware of this creative maneuvering, parents usually assume that the medication has lost its effectiveness. Actually the only thing the child has outgrown is his willingness to take the medication.

Teenagers want to be like everyone else, and taking medication separates them from the pack. Even when a teenager is given the opportunity to take one time-released pill in the privacy of his own room, the opposition often continues. Many such boys and girls seem to develop very strong negative feelings about any foreign substance or medication in their bodies.

What a wonderful side effect it would be if taking medication for ADHD "immunized" your child against drug and alcohol abuse later. Of course no one means to suggest that. By definition, many ADHD youngsters are impulsive and find it difficult to follow rules. Add to that poor self-esteem and you have conditions ripe for a child to be vulnerable to peer pressure and drug use. If that is the case, effective treatment for ADHD, which may include medication, open communication and careful supervision, remains your family's best safeguard against drug abuse.

Will my child outgrow the need for medication?

For some youngsters the answer to this question is yes. As they pass through puberty and mature, these boys and girls appear to undergo certain physiological changes that either decrease their need for medication, undermine its effectiveness or both. This process may be accompanied by a decrease in hyperactivity, but usually the problems with inattention and impulsiveness remain.

Other children need medication throughout adolescence. Because of their changes in body size and weight, they may need a larger dose of medication to concentrate as well in school. On the other hand, as skills in coping with the symptoms of ADHD are learned and as class size and schedule change so that the student has more control over his school day, some ADHD youngsters find they are able to function as well on a smaller dosage. Still we have seen seniors in high school as well as college students who need medication to survive in school. Once these individuals were out of school and had chosen occupations that matched their cognitive tempo, they got along without any medication.

Should my child take medication
only during school hours?

Your child should take medication only when it is needed. The appropriate question here is when he needs it.

For many ADHD youngsters, that seems to mean during school hours, because that is the time when they must concentrate the most. Of course, after an exhausting day at school or work, anyone's ability to concentrate is drained. The result in many homes are evenings when parents and children interact over a battleground called homework. If your child's attention is aided by an afternoon dose without negative side effects, then you should consider doing this regularly.

Other activities also require self-control and concentration. From playing ball to attending concerts, the difference between success and disaster for the ADHD child is sometimes the timing of his medication. If the child can function well over the weekends and on holidays without medication, fine. If he feels better about himself on medication and you feel better about him, too, and there are no medical or other reasons why he should not take it, then why not gain the benefits medication brings? You know that the characteristics of your child's behavior that led to a diagnosis of ADHD are the same ones that often lead to negative interaction between you and your child and your child and others. Medication, along with behavioral interventions, is needed by some children seven days a week in order for them to relate well with others and to have a chance to function happily.

*How do I know if my child
is on the right medication?*

Once the decision is made, the only way to tell if a medication is the right one for your child is to try it. Most children are started on one of the short-acting stimulant medications such as methylphenidate (Ritalin) or d-amphetamines (Dexedrine). These medications have the advantage of reaching peak effectiveness quickly, so that they may be taken close to the time needed. They are water soluble and out of the body within a few hours. These characteristics make it easier to adjust the dosage the child needs over days or weeks. There are drawbacks to the quick action, particularly when a child would benefit from a more constant effect. Since the medications must be taken more often, some children become embarrassed by taking additional doses at school.

In recent years, time-released versions of the short-acting stimulants have been developed by the drug companies. Ritalin SR and Dexedrine Spansule have the advantage of lasting up to eight hours as opposed to two or three. Obviously this means some children are able to take one pill before leaving home in the morning, so they are much more willing to cooperate. For the older child and teen, this one factor protects self-esteem. A disadvantage of this form of the medication is that it takes much longer to reach its peak effect and often never achieves as strong an effect as the child needs at critical times. Some children augment the time-release version with a dose of the regular form of the drug as needed during the day.

As we have discussed, some children do not do well on either the fast-acting or the slow-release version of the stimulants. The response may not be strong enough, or they may show fluctuations and emotional reactions to these drugs; so alternative medications are sought. Drugs such as pemoline (Cylert) build up very gradually in the bloodstream and do not wash out quickly. It may take a week to see what effect a particular dose is having and weeks to adjust it. Nevertheless Cylert is a tremendous help to a small percentage of children.

A number of other medications are occasionally prescribed for ADHD children. These include imipramine (Tofranil), which is an antidepressant. Used sometimes with bedwetters, imipramine seems most appropriate for the anxious, depressed child who may be more distracted by his internal thoughts and feelings than for the typical developmentally ADHD child. A number of less frequently prescribed medications are thought to improve the action of the neurotransmitters in the brain. Any of these medications should be used as a last alternative, and then only with the supervision of a specialist.

What is the optimum dosage for my child?

Theoretically, somewhere between .3 and .5 milligrams of stimulant per kilogram of your child's weight is thought to give the best overall results, but since each child's metabolism and reaction pattern are different, the best dosage is the one that is appropriate for your child. We have seen some very large children react strongly to a very small dosage, and we have worked with small children who required much larger doses than anticipated to get any effect at all.

One reason it is complicated to anticipate the effect of medication on ADHD children is that these drugs not only affect each child differently, but they may affect the child's symptoms differently, as well. For one youngster, a relatively small dose may improve concentration but have a negligible impact on activity level or impulsiveness. A larger dose may decrease another's impulsiveness but also decrease social interactions and attention.

Because of variations like these, it is essential to set up a system to monitor how the medication affects the specific aspects of ADHD, you are attempting to moderate. Only in this way can your child's team—parent, teacher, therapist and physician—make appropriate decisions for your child.

■ *Monitoring System*

A good monitoring system helps you observe the effects of medication in an objective way. Of course any monitoring system is only as good as the information it collects. To create an effective system, you must have the means to collect good information in several different areas.

The first is medical monitoring. Depending on the medication prescribed for your child, only periodic checkups of vital signs, weight and height may be needed. For most stimulant medications, reviews every six months along with the normal medical tests conducted as part of your child's yearly physical are sufficient. For some of the longer-acting medications, like Cylert, your child's doctor will order a periodic blood test, to ensure against adverse effects. Discuss this in advance with the doctor to set up the preferred schedule for rechecks.

In addition to any medical monitoring, you must have a way of noting the influence of the medication on your child's attention span, concentration, impulsiveness, activity level, social emotional behavior and academic performance. This kind of information will permit your child's team—parent, teacher, therapist and physician—to determine if the medication is having a positive effect and then make adjustments to optimize its effectiveness.

One source of information is already available. The types of measures used to make the original diagnosis of ADHD now offer a comparison point for your child's performance on medication. The longer questionnaires surveyed many areas of behavior. Initially the standardized score your child received allowed the doctor to compare your child to norms. When these questionnaires are administered before treatment begins and then periodically at key points during treatment, they provide valuable insights into changes in behavior. A very common order of events illustrates the sequence. As part of a comprehensive assessment, perhaps your child rated "very hyperactive" on the Conners Teacher Rating Scale. After the diagnosis is completed, he is placed on medication. Based on briefer teacher questionnaires and oral reporting by the teacher over a period of weeks, the child's dosage is increased until everyone involved feels he is doing much better. At this point it would be important to readminister the initial instrument to measure how much progress he has made on a standard measure. After it is determined that the medication is in fact having the desired effect on the problem areas defined in the initial questionnaires, you may repeat the process at the end of the school term, when there is a new schedule or other changes prompt questions.

While periodic monitoring is necessary, the crux of your feedback system is a systematic means of following your child's behavior on a regular basis. These briefer but more frequent measures allow fine adjustments in both the timing and amount of medication prescribed to be made. As you will learn in Chapters 7 through 13, daily reports will provide information you and your child's teachers and therapist can use to shape the child's progress.

The first step is to determine which behaviors will be the focus of monitoring. This will vary from child to child. If your child is rated as very restless and is frequently out of his seat, roaming the classroom, then this could be one of the behaviors you track. If inability to complete work on time is also of concern, that might be another designated behavior to count. Your physician or therapist will also want information about your child's home and school schedule in order to prescribe the time and dosage of medication.

One key element in successful monitoring is the ease of implementation of your system. If it is time-consuming and complicated, no one will follow through for very long. Obviously creating the right monitoring system takes some ingenuity, but it is feasible.

After working with many families and teachers, we have created a feedback system that is easy to use and highly informative. The Act-o-meter on the Daily Report Card shown in Figure 6.1 was derived from the familiar dials on an automobile dashboard. Immediately recognizable, it offers a simple rating system that can be adapted to the needs of many different children. The Daily Report Card provides a simple means to guide daily progress.

Since the record will be going back and forth regularly between home and school, supply all monitoring materials to the teachers. You may duplicate the charts and other forms in this book for your own use or you may use the information in Appendix A to order the charts and materials we discuss.

The report card in Figure 6.1 is very simple to complete. The teacher or sometimes the child colors in the book on the left side that reports how much work he completed that day. The teacher could initial the amount to verify the claim and place a line at the appropriate point on the Act-o-meter to indicate how active the child was. A card like this takes a few seconds to complete and provides a basic but credible summary for the day. If your child's memory for bringing the report home is recorded and rewarded, no matter what it says, then he will learn to comply. In fact when the card itself is the ticket the child needs to do any of his favorite after-school activities, he is much more likely to remember it. For maximum results, a child should always earn some privilege or reward for bringing home

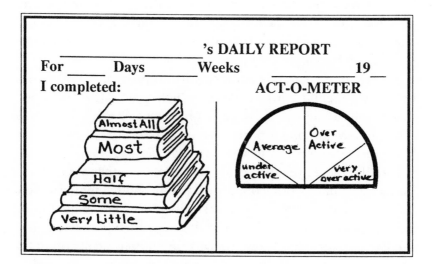

FIGURE 6.1
Daily Report Card

a completed card and extra reinforcement for improvements in ratings on the card. When a child fails to bring home his card, do not overreact. If it is a rare occurrence, simply tell him he has another opportunity to return it tomorrow. Missing whatever privilege or reward might have been earned should serve as an inducement to prompt his memory. To increase the number of days that a child remembers to return his card, you may keep a tally of days in a row he remembers, then reward an increasing total.

Every system needs a backup. There will be times when the daily monitoring system falls apart. Nevertheless, monitoring information must be collected and communicated between school, home, and doctors. A chart such as the one shown in Figure 6.2 can be used to transmit relevant information in a very time-efficient manner. Initially and at key points, this chart can be used to collect information on a daily basis; at other times weekly averages may be recorded. For ease of use, the back of the form should be conveniently set up as a mailer. A number of these preaddressed mailers will ease the teacher's job.

Variations of the report forms can also be used at home. Instead of recording how many times a child gets out of his seat at school, you could track the number of times he gets out of his chair at the dinner table. Completion of homework rather than work at school can be monitored similarly.

Review of the summary tracking forms provides a visual record of your child's performance, which your doctor or other professionals can use to judge the influence of medication and other interventions on particular aspects of ADHD. Based on the information, new interventions may be suggested.

Finally, there are other kinds of information that are helpful. Collect and date work samples that your child completes. You may be surprised to discover vast differences in the quality of your child's handwriting during the school day. Analyzing the quality of your child's handwriting on and off medication and at different times of the day provides valuable information about the effects of medication on visual-motor functioning.

In addition to quality of written work it is often a good idea to have the teacher save all of your child's work for particular days. Provide her with an accordion file marked by days. For each date, ask the teacher to list what the child should have done that day. This will permit you to calculate the percentage of assignments your child completed that day. A review of the actual work samples will allow the professionals you are working with to assess the time of day and kinds of work that are the most troublesome. This need not be done frequently but is very useful when changes in medication or programming are considered. On several occasions, children with whom we have worked were suddenly rated as more inattentive. It would have been easy to assume they needed to change medication. By reviewing their work load, we could see that the problems oc-

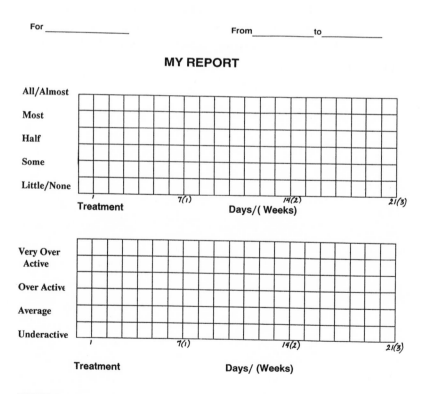

FIGURE 6.2
My Summary Report

curred at times when the effects of medication were waning. All that was needed was a change in the timing of the medication. In other cases careful analysis of children's work made it clear the student was having specific problems with subject matter. Medication alone cannot overcome such learning problems or fill in skill deficits.

The choice to use medication is an important one. As you can see, starting medication is not the only decision to be made. Careful monitoring of your child's reactions to medication and of changes in his behavior is the only way this part of your child's treatment program can be evaluated. We emphasize the fact that medication is never the sole treatment program for the ADHD child. What you do beyond medication is what makes the decision to administer stimulant medication really worthwhile. The effects of medication are temporary; the effects of instruction and intervention can last a lifetime. Medication can help those children who respond well to it reap the benefits of other forms of treatment.

7.
Controlling Activity Level

*T*he only thing most ADHD children know about being still is what their parents tell them: "Be still. Why can't you be still?" While other children sit through meals or remain quietly in their seats at school, these youngsters wiggle, rock in their chairs or get up and down twenty times. At their best they squirm through the moments. Other ADHD children find it less difficult to control their physical activity, but their minds jump around. Focusing and unfocusing, darting from object to sound, their attention is controlled by the environment. Perplexingly, at any second, the typical ADHD child can become immersed in observing an object or glued to a television monitor.

This then is the dilemma. The ADHD child is unaware that

he can take control of his reactions—to be less active or to filter out distractions. While other children naturally turn their motion on and off, consciously focus attention and resist the urge to get up, these youngsters must learn how.

In this chapter, beginning with games like Statue and Beat the Clock, you will learn ways to help your child control his movement, set the idle lower and put a governor on impulses so he can gain control over his body movements and attention span. It takes training, but after some initial success, he will soon recognize control as a desirable accomplishment. With further practice your child will define the rules and learn how to behave appropriately in a variety of situations. The goal is not an easy one for your child to achieve, but it is possible.

While other children seem to know when and how to sit still, the ADHD child does not appear to know that he can be motionless. One particular example, typical of many children we see, highlights this point and shows how the Statue game can work with even the most active youngster.

Seven-year-old Ronnie was a perpetual-motion machine temporarily perched between his parents as they filled out forms in our waiting room. From pillow to book and back to Mom, he jumped incessantly across the furniture. Observations of him in our waiting area provided a piece of the diagnostic puzzle.

As Ronnie walked down the hall he strummed his fingers against the wallpaper and darted into an office, talking nonstop the entire time. None of this is particularly unusual. Nor was Ronnie's response to the stopwatch we showed him. He was immediately interested, starting and stopping the second hand several times before we asked him if he would like to play a game called Statue.

We asked Ronnie if he had ever seen any statues. He replied he had seen the Statue of Liberty. After displaying a few pictures of other famous statues, we asked Ronnie if he could strike a pose like a statue. We took instant photos of the ones he depicted. Adding a new dimension to the game, we asked Ronnie how long he thought he could sit completely still. He boasted, "Sixty-seven minutes." Suggesting that might be too long for anyone, ten seconds was offered as a realistic compromise. Confidently Ronnie got into position and started the timer.

On his first try, Ronnie posed for seventeen seconds. Any blinking or minor movements of the face or limbs were ignored. As you can see in the Staircase to Success Chart shown in Figure 7.1, Ronnie's score improved on each attempt—from thirty-five to sixty to ninety seconds. By the time his parents came in, Ronnie was edging towards a new world's record for Statue of two minutes. His parents were amazed and Ronnie looked pretty pleased himself.

Over the next few weeks, Ronnie's parents played the game with him several times until he could sit fairly consistently for approximately five minutes. Every trial was not a success, but more often than not Ronnie made his target time. His efforts were always praised, but when he was not successful his parents told him not to worry, he could try again tomorrow. His interest was maintained and he was a willing participant in training.

Statue is the first step in teaching your child how to gain control over his body. In the rest of the chapter we will present the directions for three types of activities you will use to teach your child to control his activity level.

■ Learning to Play Statue

The game Statue will first help your child become aware of his body movements and then teach him to control the urge to move. For the game you will need:

- A stopwatch or watch with a start/stop function. For younger children a simple digital timer that shows seconds is best. A more complicated sports-type stopwatch or inexpensive chronograph watch may hold added appeal for the older child.
- A clipboard on which to keep record sheets and directions. Some children enjoy displaying their record for all to see, while others prefer privacy. You know your child best.
- Pictures of statues from books or magazines.

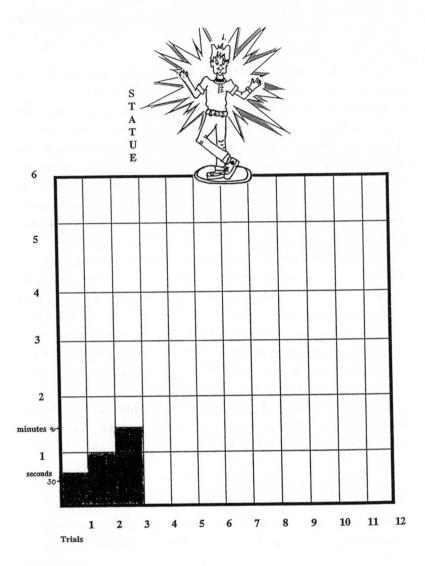

FIGURE 7.1

Ronnie's Staircase to Success Chart

- Copies of the Statue Staircase to Success Chart pictured in Figure 7.2. You may make as many copies of this chart as you wish for your own personal use.
- The Point Bank. The Point Bank may be a chart, collection bank or any visual record such as the one shown in Figure 7.3, which allows the child to collect and save the points he earns. You may copy Figure 7.3 for your personal use or order materials from the address in Appendix A.
- A pen or marker to record times and color in the graph.
- A chair in which your child can comfortably sit with his feet flat on the floor. It's essential that his feet not dangle.

Begin by acknowledging that you realize it is sometimes difficult for your child to sit still. This game will help him learn how to control the impulse to move. You may want to use one of the stories in Chapter 4 to help you.

- Teach your child how to pose like a statue. Show your child the pictures of the statues you have collected. Talk about the guards at Buckingham Palace, who stand so silently as people attempt to get their attention. Then ask your child if he can stand at attention like a palace guard. Tell him you will attempt to distract him, so he must work hard to maintain a steady gaze and ignore you as you wave your hands and jump around. Make a few funny faces to try to throw him off guard. Now switch places and let him tempt you. An older child might prefer striking military positions, like standing at attention.

Demonstrate various poses and have your child mimic you. How about George Washington gazing across the Delaware, the Statue of Liberty looking out to sea, or Abraham Lincoln saluting his soldiers? Strike your pose, hold it while your child copies it, then let your child take the lead.

- Help your child become aware of his impulses to move by playing Catch Me If You Can. Sit in chairs across from each other. Your child's seat must be at a height that permits him to place both feet comfortably on the floor. Tell your child to watch you carefully, catching each movement you make with your body, aside from breathing and slight changes in facial expression. Exaggerate your movements before becoming more

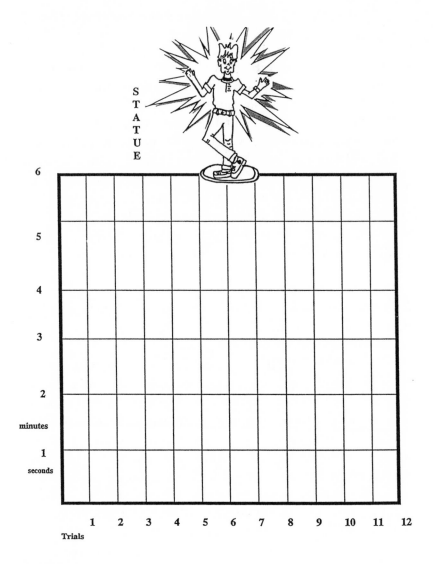

FIGURE 7.2

Statue Staircase to Success Chart

FIGURE 7.3
My Point Bank

subtle so that he can easily catch you. Reverse roles so that you point out his obvious violations, but avoid being so strict you discourage participation.

• Encourage your child to be aware of how stillness and the urge to move feel. Ask him to close his eyes and concentrate on the parts of his body. How do the muscles feel as he sits quietly? What do the muscles feel like when he has the need to move them? Ask him to point to a body part he senses the need to move before he moves it.

■ *The World's Record Trials*

• Define a beginning goal. Show your child the Statue Staircase to Success Chart and explain that he will be recording how long he is able to sit without moving. Hand him a stopwatch, affording him the chance to manipulate it before you begin training. After a few minutes, ask your child how long he thinks he can sit still, eventually setting a reasonable goal for the first trial. His initial attempt can be as brief as a few seconds, for success is the key.

• Record and reward your child's performance. Any exercise is more palatable if you dress it up, so with great flourish praise every attempt. One point is earned for matching old records, two points for breaking a record. Points earned can be tallied on a Point Bank, such as the one in Figure 7.3, or you may use one of the other options outlined in Chapter 3. Highlight increments of progress with such comments as "That's great. You made it to twenty-three seconds the first time, then thirty-eight, and now fifty-five. Are you ready for a new world's record? Do you think you can hit sixty seconds?"

• Proceed slowly. Do not worry about rapid progress; your child's been a mover for years. Each additional second is another success, but do avoid long practice sessions. It is better to stop if he tires or becomes bored than to wear out his enthusiasm.

• Repeat the game intermittently, making sure breaks of several days occur between sessions. Continue with Statue until your child can sit still for approximately five minutes fairly consistently. Practice sessions should be kept brief. It may take several weeks or more to reach that goal. Working parents can also work practice time into the schedule in the evenings and during weekends. Along the way, enthusiastically praise his progress but downplay lesser achievements. Even Olympic athletes are not successful each time out of the starting gate, but they are not considered losers.

■ *Playing Beat the Clock*

Learning to control his activity level, as your child did with the Statue game, is a real accomplishment. Yet it is of little use unless the skill can be generalized and extended to other settings, where being able to control oneself improves the quality of the experience for everyone. With Beat the Clock, your child will learn how to match his body motion to the requirements of the situation.

It is not unusual for a family to tell us they have never completed a meal with all members of the family present at the table at one time. Since dinner at a restaurant offers no relief either, many parents of ADHD youngsters avoid anyplace without a fast-food bar. A trip to the mall or, heaven forbid, sitting through a religious service requires the endurance of a professional athlete. You can begin to bridge this gap with Beat the Clock and continue with Endurance Training. With these games, your child will learn to resist the urge to move, get up, wiggle and fidget so that he can sit through a meal without multiple excursions and interruptions. Learning to stay by your side as you visit a neighbor or tour the mall is not magic. It requires you to teach him skills you have assumed your child should naturally know. In the process, your expectations will change. Your child's view of himself will undergo a remarkable transformation, just as eight-year-old Seth's did.

Seth came running into our office, his face bearing a big grin, eager to report that he had successfully made it through twenty-three minutes at a pizzeria without getting out of his seat one time. Significantly, he had beaten the urge to jump up seven times. He was confident he was ready to return to one of Mom and Dad's favorite restaurants, which had been off-limits to him for a while.

Like Seth, once your child is able to sit still during Statue for five minutes, he is ready for Beat the Clock. Begin with a simple situation that occurs often at home and affords many natural opportunities for practice. Since dinner time is a natural we have used it as the sample situation. Play situations in which your child simply needs to learn to remain longer with a single activity are also good.

• The purpose of Beat the Clock. In Statue your child was taught not to move at all. That is effective for a learning experience, but it is not a realistic long-term behavioral goal. With Beat the Clock, you reteach your child appropriate behavior for each setting. Often a child learns a behavior in one place but does not practice it in other settings. Although your child knows not to interrupt you when you are on the phone, he may not show the same restraint when you are having a conversation with others in your living room or if you meet someone at the mall. Many children, but especially ADHD children, must be taught to generalize one skill to a variety of situations.

Each place you go and each activity you participate in has its own unspoken set of rules. Most of us learn these rules by watching others, picking up cues from the environment and refining our skills through indirect instruction and the feedback we receive. Again, the ADHD child requires a more direct approach. Through the activities in Beat the Clock, your child will be exposed to the rules of a situation and learn the appropriate behaviors for a successful experience.

• After selecting your target situation, define the rules. Rather than delivering a complete laundry list of rules, develop them with your child. Including your child in the process of rule development is a necessity with the older child and important motivation for the younger one. The more input your child has, the greater his understanding and acceptance of the rules you develop will be. In addition, through the discussion, you are modeling the process you want your child to adopt when he enters a new situation. To define the rules for your situation, start with these questions:

What kind of behavior is appropriate?

How are other people behaving in the situation?

What cues are available that tell someone how to act?

Together construct statements that describe reasonable behaviors for the situation. As you talk with your child keep in mind:

The rules should be framed positively.

Use the child's words to describe the desired behavior.

The rules should reflect minimum standards in the beginning.

The scenario for a discussion about dinner time might take the following course. Ask your child how long he thinks a typical evening meal might take at your house. Where is the best place for everyone to eat? Why? How do we eat? What are some appropriate dinner-time rules? If your child suggests, "Don't run around the table," you might respond, "I know we shouldn't run around the table, but what should you do instead?" Keeping in mind that your child must build upon success, "sitting in your seat through the entire meal" might be difficult to achieve immediately, but a shorter time frame might be possible.

Three rules devised by a family with a seven-year-old daughter include:

1. Stay at the table until you are given permission to leave.
2. Sit with your bottom on the chair and your feet on the floor.
3. Use silverware to eat.

Often children become so involved in the process they identify too many rules. That gives you the opportunity to be the kind person who eliminates a few. Consider any reluctance to reduce the number of rules as a positive sign. Ultimately you want your child to internalize the rule-governing process so that he feels a responsibility to adhere to accepted standards of behavior.

 • Keep the rules as simple as possible. Select a few important positive statements, informing your child that others can be added as he progresses. Also avoid emphasizing a time element in the rules. For example, Rule 1, "Stay in your seat until you are given permission to leave," enables you gradually to increase the requirements as the child gains control over his dinner-time behavior.

Write the rules on clockcards such as the one shown in Figure 7.4. A small card works best because the child is able to carry his rules and scorekeeper to the table or wherever he is playing. That places the responsibility for remembering the rules right where it should be—on your child.

- Role-play the game. Before you play Beat the Clock at meal-time, give it a quiet run-through in a setting where there are few distractions. You will need your clockcards, a stopwatch or timer with a second-hand feature, a colored marker, and the Point Bank. Beginning with Rule 1, demonstrate several behav-

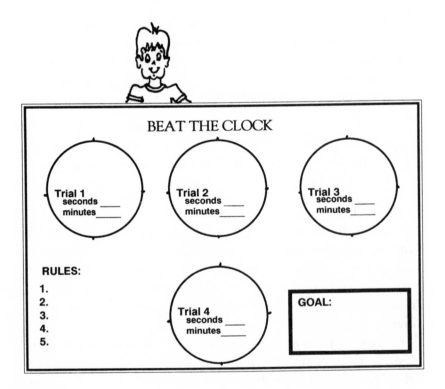

FIGURE 7.4
Clockcard

iors, letting your child identify which are examples of following the rule. For sitting at the table, you might sit halfway off the seat, resting most of your weight on one foot at the side of the chair. Then sit with your seat on the chair and your hands in your lap. Or take turns demonstrating some acceptable and nonacceptable rule following. It is okay to have a little fun, as long as your child understands which behaviors are within the limits and the jesting does not get out of hand.

While your child pretends to be at the dinner table, say "Go" and start the timer. Without being too strict, call time as soon as a rule is clearly violated. Help your child read his time, record it on the clockcard and reset the watch. Give him positive feedback on both the length of the achievement and which rules he kept. Or ask him which rule he broke. If he resisted the urge to break a rule, inquire about how he accomplished that: "Did you want to move earlier? How did you stop yourself?" Question how he might deal with this impulse during the next round so he can extend his time. Again, regardless of how brief his success, praise your child. If he feels that it was not good enough, reassure him that he will have other chances to play Beat the Clock.

Inform your child each time he breaks his record. As before, matching the previous time is worth one point and a new record is worth two. Continue with a few trials, ending the training session before boredom sets in.

- Start Beat the Clock in the real setting. Review the rules and the use of the clockcard. Taking into account your child's age and wishes, find the right moment to explain the game to the rest of the family. If the other children in the family want charts of their own, design them to be used at other times of the day with other behaviors. Your ADHD child should compete only with himself.

- Play the game one time to set the initial goal. In subsequent trials, the game begins with the last goal achieved. The child marks the goal on the clockcard for each trial as it begins. Praise his effort during each trial. Point out which rules he is keeping, with comments like, "You are sitting in your chair the right way; that's Rule 1," or "I like the way you are using your silverware." After a while he will have the rules memorized, so that all you need do to compliment his effort is mention a number or make a hand signal. Silent signals, such as a pull on the ear, add a game-like quality and alleviate teasing or embarrassment.

▪ Give time cues during the game. "You've made it to six minutes, only two more to your goal." As long as it does not distract him from the task or interfere with his pace, your youngster might enjoy keeping track of his own time. Or you can designate a set of hand signals that maintain privacy yet identify the time.

▪ Continue the game until your child decides to stop or a rule is broken. On the clockcard, record only the time reached, using a new clock face for each trial. Designate a new record with a star. Each time your child meets his goal or exceeds it, he should earn two points. On Walt's clockcard in Figure 7.5, you can see he marked forty-two seconds in the first trial, one minute three seconds for trial two, and one minute thirty for the third round.

Handle any disappointment and complaints matter-of-factly, reminding your child that there will be plenty of other opportunities for him to establish a new record. As the official referee, define the rules that were met, then ask your child to mark the new goal on the next clock and go for it.

Review your child's clockcards at the conclusion of each session. As practice ends, total the number of points earned and transfer them to his point bank.

▪ Gradually increase the requirements. As your child's behavior improves and he approaches reasonable time limits for the situation, gradually add more rules or strengthen the initial ones, involving your child in the decision as you did previously. This is another way for him to measure his progress. He may be ready for the rules you omitted originally. Or by now, he may be able to sit at the table for a designated number of minutes consistently, making it appropriate for you to set a minimum sitting time. Alternatively, you may decide that ten minutes spent adhering to five rules is better than twenty minutes adhering to three. New challenges are a sign of progress.

Add the new and/or improved rules to a new clockcard, then set a new goal and play the game again. For example, the rules might be increased to five now, including keeping the chair itself still and making appropriate sounds at the dinner table. Rule 3 might be strengthened to include no playing with silverware.

• Try Beat the Clock outside the home. If you were working on dinner time, your child has now succeeded in sitting through meals at home, so with modest expectation, you are ready to face the outside world again. Do not start with the fanciest restaurant you know or the one with the worst record for service. Suggest several places your child would enjoy, but let him make the final choice.

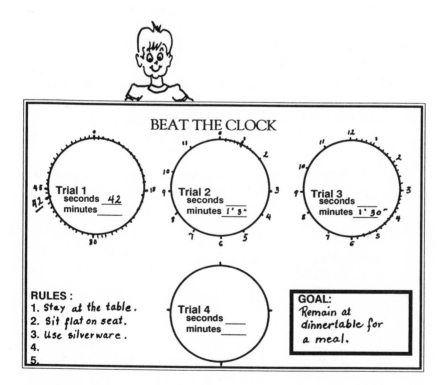

FIGURE 7.5
Walt's Clockcard

Before your first visit, create rules for eating at the restaurant together. Avoid taking an entourage. Your child may think it is more of an event if the two of you go alone initially.

Use a clockcard to record your child's times in the new setting, using the signals and procedures that worked so well at home. Be sure to reinforce your child for all successes during the visit.

- The same process will work anywhere. Define the rules together before reaching your destination. Define the goal and record progress. Over time, signals can be phased out, but don't forget to praise those hard-earned new behaviors.

■ *Endurance Training*

With Statue and Beat the Clock your child learned, first, that he could control his activity level and, second, that in each setting there are particular behaviors that are appropriate. As he recognizes more cues in the environment he will need less prompting as to how he should behave.

With endurance training you are going for the long haul—strengthening the skills and stretching the time your child is able to sit still in a variety of settings. You don't expect him to be a perfect angel; you just want him to act like a typical child his age.

- Think about the long-term results you hope to achieve with your child. Make a list of the places and settings where he still has the most trouble behaving appropriately now. Prioritize the list. Walt's family's list read:

1. religious services
2. car
3. movies
4. doctor's office
5. restaurants

- Talk with your child about appropriate behaviors for the first setting. Just as you did with Beat the Clock, define the rules of behavior for the situation. List them on a clockcard.
- Set endurance goals with your child. In Beat the Clock the

goals were based on time, but there are few time guarantees in the real world. With endurance training the time frame is matched to events in the setting. First, discuss the situation in terms of your ultimate expectations. For example, Walt's parents wanted him to be able to sit through an entire religious service. Other children the same age as Walt sit quietly through the service, and they wanted their son to behave similarly. This then became the final endurance goal.

▪ Divide the situation into manageable parts. Walt's parents had to begin with a shorter time period because Walt was not ready to sit through an entire service. Together they broke down the situation into time segments Walt could comfortably endure. That would vary for each child. For Walt a reasonable set of time goals was determined to be:

First, sit in the service through opening prayers.
Second, sit through the service until the sermon.
Third, sit through the service until the end of the sermon.
Last, sit through the service until it is complete.

On a modified clockcard like the one shown in Figure 7.6, these time goals were entered as endurance goals. The goal Walt was working on now was circled.

▪ Initiate endurance training in the real setting. As you did with Beat the Clock, role-play the behaviors at home before you enter the real situation. When you begin endurance training in the real situation, set a goal for the first day. For Walt it was to sit quietly through opening prayers. As he sat, his parents signaled the rules he was following and how much longer to the goal.

When your child reaches the goal, mark it on the clock face and praise his success. Once more, meeting the goal is worth two points for the Point Bank. If your child works toward the goal but finds it impossible to achieve, the time frame was too long. On the next trial, lower the expectations. If your child clearly misbehaves, remove him from the situation and fine him two points. Continued acting-out should be followed with an appropriate consequence like time-out. Time-out should be conducted in a boring place where the child remains for a time period equal to one minute for each year of age. Thinking this way, a ten-year-old would stay in time-out for ten minutes.

• Set the goal for each trial in the situation. Walt's parents were pleased when their son achieved his second goal and was able to remain in his seat until the start of the sermon. Deciding that this was a reasonable goal to maintain for a while, they continued to award Walt two points when he met the goal. When his clockcard is filled with successfully met goals, your child should earn a bonus of five points to add to his point bank.

• Continue endurance training at a reasonable pace until the ultimate goal is achieved. Eventually your child will meet the endurance goals. It may take longer for some children than

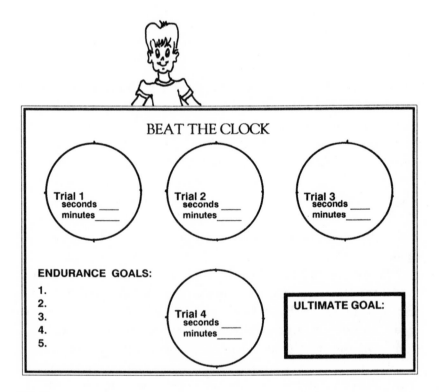

FIGURE 7.6
Clockcard with Endurance Goals

others. Working parents may have to limit expectations to fit the delays in the practice schedule. Do not get discouraged. If you reach a plateau, be satisfied for a while. Work on other skills, returning to this one at a later date. Working on his impulsiveness, on relaxation training or on other behaviors may give sitting still a boost.

8

.

Calmness
Training

"*I*f he could
just run off his excess energy, he'd calm down," is the kind of
wishful thinking echoed by many parents of ADHD children.
While any child may profit from exercise and breaks in the
schedule, these activities don't automatically decrease the
ADHD child's activity level or bring him back to task. In fact,
rather than depleting energy, extra activity appears to unleash
it in some youngsters. Like a top primed to spin, the more he
runs and jumps, the more wound up the ADHD child becomes.
The result is a child who must be calmed down since he is
unlikely to be able to do it himself. That is the problem in a
nutshell. So, how do you help a child achieve enough self-control to be able to calm himself?

Many parents attempt a balancing act, aspiring to maintain a calm attitude with controlled activities, low noise level, and few surprises. They approach each situation in a preventive mode. The precautions are commendable, but exhausting. What is worse, the outcome is tenuous at best. The mother of six-year-old Jake summed this up well when she said, "If I could be in control all the time with every odd in my favor, there would still be the doorbell ringing, a friend dropping over or a dog running across the yard that would set Jake into action."

ADHD children do not handle the unexpected very well. Transitions from one activity to another pose an ongoing obstacle with the threat the child will become overexcited. If he is fatigued, then he is more susceptible to overstimulation and less able to concentrate.

Relaxation training offers a partial solution to these problems. In this chapter, we will focus on how you can use relaxation training with your child anywhere you go. Of immense benefit when practiced regularly, relaxation training can help your child fall asleep, reduce his fear in a new or trying situation, keep cool in the midst of an argument and overcome test anxiety. By the way, relaxation training can also pay off for you in many ways: increased energy, less perceived stress, and greater self-control, to name a few.

Relaxation training is not a magic potion, yet you may experience the enthusiasm other advocates sustain after you try it. These techniques are not new. Some methods, like yoga and meditation, have been practiced for centuries. Progressive relaxation training, first developed by Dr. Edmund Jacobson in the 1930s, involves the progressive and continuous flexing and relaxing of each muscle group in the body until the total body reaches a state of equilibrium. Very easy to learn, it is a skill almost everyone can develop.

An advantage of relaxation training is that it requires little excess paraphernalia. Biofeedback training also has merit, but finding instruction and applying the new skill in different settings are both complicated. By contrast, once your child completes the Statue game in Chapter 7 and is able to sit calmly for several minutes, he will be ready to proceed with relaxation training. Recognize, though, that as with brushing one's teeth and maintaining one's personal hygiene, few children immediately recognize the inherent benefit of relaxation training. You may want to use a little reinforcement to increase cooperation. Instructions for giving points are included in the game directions, but for additional information refer to Chapter 3. The steps outlined in this chapter will help put your child in a relaxed frame of mind.

■ *Getting into a Relaxed Statue Position*

Have your child sit comfortably in a chair or sofa. The back of the seat should be high enough to support the child's head. It is best if your child's feet rest on the floor, which may be difficult to accomplish with small children. Arms should rest easily by his sides with the palms of the hands lying on the seat. Sit facing your child, so she can easily mirror the motions you demonstrate.

When your child is in position, ask him to freeze for a short period of time. Praise his success and tell him he has earned his first point. Inform him that this is only the beginning. There are more points for him to earn if he concentrates and watches you as you demonstrate the relaxation procedures.

BEGIN THE GREAT YAWN FEST

• "Bet I can make you yawn" starts the game. Show your child how to fake a big yawn with your mouth wide open, your eyes squeezed tightly shut and your nose wrinkled. Hold this position for a few seconds, inhale deeply through your mouth, then suddenly exhale and sigh, closing your mouth so it remains only slightly open and relaxed. Your eyes and nose will naturally return to normal, and you may feel a warm glow or tingling after repeating this routine several times. It is quite likely you will yawn for real at some point. Congratulate your child and tell him he's earned another point for paying attention.

• Ask your child to repeat the yawning routine. He will probably think it is silly, but that is okay. He may say he is not sleepy and that is fine too. Tell him to fake it so he can earn a point.

The power of suggestion is amazing. Just as you did, most children will begin to yawn spontaneously. Joke about the fact that he is now making you feel like yawning. Turnabout is fair; mirror his yawns. Praise your child's cooperation and tell him he has earned another point.

Promoting yawning can be fun at other times, too. Try it when you are sitting around the dinner table or waiting at a red light.

GOING BELLY UP

• Teach your child diaphragm breathing. Belly up is going to gain a new meaning with this round of exercise. Begin with a good yawn.

Place one hand, palm down, over your belly button. Assuming the same position, have your child copy your actions as you both take slow easy breaths that fill the abdomen with air. As you slowly breathe in to the count of five, your abdomen should rise as it inflates with air. As you exhale, your stomach should sink. If you or your child have a problem getting the abdomen to move like this, extend your legs or stretch out on the floor. Lying on your back, you can see as well as feel the stomach rise and fall. Placing a book on the stomach will help to promote the correct movement. Remember to breathe slowly but not too deeply. You want to produce full, easy breaths rather than short, tense chest breaths. For belly or slow breathing your child earns one point and additional ones for doing a good job.

• Combine the big yawn and belly breathing. Once your child has mastered the basic breathing, have him combine a big yawn with a belly breath, ending with his eyes closed and his hands resting on his stomach. Ask him to practice slow breathing for several minutes, using the timer to let him know when he has reached his goal. This earns him an extra point on his relaxation-training chart.

• Add another dimension to relaxation training. Ask your child to yawn several times. In this relaxed mood ask him to imagine a favorite place, such as the beach or a mountain scene.

Talk him through an enjoyable time at one of these places, recounting the fun things he did, like riding waves, floating on a raft in the cool water or lying on the warm sand. Can he feel the heat of the sun or the gentle breeze? Let him lie there for a few moments basking in the memories. During other practice sessions, you may extend the imaginary trip.

▪ Make a practice tape. Some children enjoy using a cassette tape that describes their favorite scene in detail. The advantage of the tape is obvious: it is available when you are not! In addition, it provides a means for your child to accept some responsiblity and use the tape to relax and unwind. Promote initiative by awarding one point each time he practices.

LOOSEN UP ARMS AND HANDS

Return to a relaxed state by practicing slow breathing for a few minutes with your child. Instruct him to maintain the same position with his eyes open.

▪ Teach your child how to relax his upper limbs. Ask your child to imagine you are both marionettes whose arms and legs are attached to the ceiling by strings that control their movement. Next, model what happens when a string is raised. What happens to each limb? What happens if the string is cut? Role-play each possibility until you are sure your child understands the concept.

▪ Focus on the hand and arms. Ask your child to do as you do. Make a fist, then slowly extend your arm with closed palm facing downward. Hold that position for several seconds. Instruct your child to take a deep breath and when you say, "Relax," imagine the string is cut, immediately dropping the opened hand to the seat.

Repeat the arm exercises three times, alternating between the left and right sides of the body. Your child should earn one point for each set of repetitions. With each set, the arms may feel a little heavier, warmer or tingly. You may suggest these sensations but it is okay if either of you does not feel all of them.

LIMBER LEGS

▪ Teach your child to relax the legs. Instruct your child to duplicate your actions as you lift your right leg. *(If you or your child has back problems or this exercise causes any back discomfort, then skip this step or lift your leg only as far off the floor as is comfortable.)* Hold the position for a count of ten or fifteen, suggesting that the leg is like that of a puppet suspended by a string. Hold the position as the leg becomes very heavy. Take a big breath, say "Relax," and drop it as you exhale. Repeat this exercise, alternating legs until each limb has been tensed and relaxed three times. Award one point per repetition.

ALL THE STEPS TOGETHER

▪ Lead your child through the combined yawning, breathing, imagining and tensing/relaxing the large muscles. The practice sessions should be brief and conducted every other day at most. Each practice is worth three points.

▪ Find times to practice. Many parents find that bedtime is the perfect time to rehearse. The child does not feel cheated out of another activity and the exercises naturally help him unwind. If a bed is used, have your child lie down, lifting his arms and legs off the bed before he drops them.

▪ Give encouragement and praise freely. The chart in Figure 8.1 and a reward program such as the one outlined in Chapter 3 can be used to promote your child's cooperation. If your child resists an activity on a particular evening, try another time. It is best to avoid power struggles.

▪ Model the relaxation exercises yourself. Do not underestimate the impact of your modeling. Make a point of telling your child that you are going to your room for fifteen minutes to practice your relaxation skills. Let him see you going through the paces at other times. If the exercises help you to feel better, share that experience. Relaxation training may well improve your ability to cope, too.

■ *Spread the Feeling*

- Encourage your child to use his new relaxation skills. It is no secret, the goal of practicing these techniques is for you and your child to be able to use them to relax at will. As your child gains skill with the exercises, encourage him to try them at bedtime, when he comes home from school or when he is upset

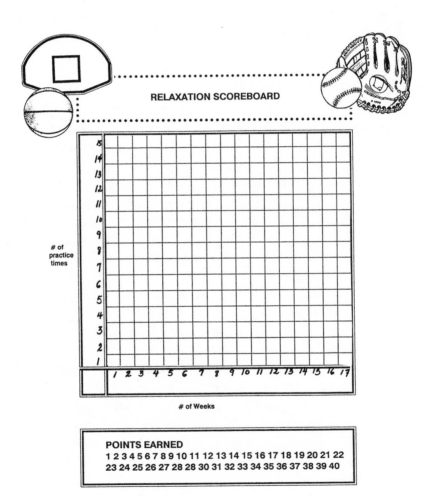

RELAXATION SCOREBOARD

# of practice times

# of Weeks

POINTS EARNED
1 2 3 4 5 6 7 8 9 10 11 12 13 14 15 16 17 18 19 20 21 22
23 24 25 26 27 28 28 30 31 32 33 34 35 36 37 38 39 40

FIGURE 8.1
Relaxation Scoreboard

or tense. Reinforce him with praise and points when you see him taking a deep breath or trying to relax his limbs.

▪ Demonstrate ways to inconspicuously apply the techniques while sitting in the car or restaurant. Make it a game to see how quietly you can practice without others' taking note. Of course, your child cannot lift and drop his arms without being seen, but he could tightly grip the arm of a chair, then let his arm fall quietly into his lap. Yawning and deep breathing easily accommodate to various situations as long as the actor is not too big of a ham. A yawn with a fist covering the mouth can be made to look very natural, as long as it is performed silently.

▪ Prompt your child to try these exercises in other situations. Extra reinforcement may spawn increased impetus. Copy the chart in Figure 8.1 and keep track of the number of times your child practices his relaxation skills, or if your child prefers, have him keep his own record. Each practice session should earn him one point; five points should be awarded for beating the previous week's practice record. Older youngsters also respond to a contract such as the one in Figure 8.2. With practice, over time, your child will recognize the benefits of relaxation training and begin to employ it naturally as he proceeds through the day.

TEAM CONTRACT

The players are : ______________________________
(child)

____
(parent)

______________________________(child) **will practice relaxation in**

____(situation).

Each time ______________(child) **practices, he or she will earn**

______________**points.**

Number of sessions:
Week 1 1 2 3 4 5 6 7 8 9 10 11 12 13 14 15 16 17 18 19 20
Week 2 1 2 3 4 5 6 7 8 9 10 11 12 13 14 15 16 17 18 19 20
Week 3 1 2 3 4 5 6 7 8 9 10 11 12 13 14 15 16 17 18 19 20

Points earned: 1 2 3 4 5 6 7 8 9 10 11 12 13 14 15 16 17 18 19 20
21 22 23 24 25 26 27 28 29 30 31 32 33 34 35 36 37 38 39 40 41 42
43 44 45 46 47 48 49 50 51 52 53 54 55 56 57 58 59 60 61 62 63 64

______________________ ______________________
child **Parent**

____
date

FIGURE 8.2
Relaxation Contract

9.

Impulse Control Training

On many occasions
Speak First/Act First—Think Later is the motto of ADHD youngsters. From blurting out in the classroom to jumping the gun in
sporting events, their impulsiveness constantly sets these
youngsters on courses that get them into trouble. Beyond deeds,
this impetuousness extends to thoughts and feelings. When the
ADHD child is happy, sad, angry or excited, you know it—immediately!

Some consequences of impulsiveness are disastrous. Children
who leap without looking can get hurt on the playground, crossing the street and in their own homes. The consequences of
impulsiveness are one of the main reasons ADHD youngsters

end up in the doctor's office or the hospital more often than their more cautious peers.

Although impulsiveness may change its form over the years, and certainly all of us are impetuous on occasion, many ADHD youngsters do not automatically outgrow this characteristic. We have worked with teens who bought used cars on a whim without once looking under the hood or taking a test drive. A particularly rash seventeen-year-old disassembled the motor of his new car without bothering to see if he could find the manual he needed to put it back together.

Over time your youngster can learn to regulate his impulses better. Learning to control his activity level, as he did in Chapter 7, and learning to calm down, as shown in Chapter 8, help, but generally the impulsiveness must be attacked directly. The need to think before one acts is a difficult concept for your child to grasp and for you to get a handle on, because thinking is an internal process. Some researchers have approached this issue by teaching cognitive strategies to the child. They do this by showing the child what he should be saying to himself—first out loud and then more quietly until he is able to contemplate internally. These cognitive behavior modification strategies may be effective for some older, more verbal ADHD children but have not proven as successful for younger or extremely active ones. In general, we take a more direct approach to self-control training.

Explain the concept of impulsiveness. Find a quiet time to discuss with your child what you mean by impulsiveness. Use several examples of occasions when he acted rashly, as well as times when his behavior indicated he had deliberated in advance. Make a list similar to the one in Figure 9.1 and record examples of both types of behavior. For Carl's list, his mother wrote, "running into the street," then next to it, "pausing at the stoplight and looking both ways." Opposite "leaving the house without his schoolbooks," an impulsive act, she listed "putting schoolbooks in book bag before leaving for school" as a well-thought-out behavior. Other examples were "interrupting a conversation" as an impulsive act and "saying excuse me and waiting to speak" as the corresponding thought-out act.

Continue the discussion by sharing examples of your own impulsive behavior and the consequences. Point out instances when having thought things through in advance led to better results. Return to the examples of impulsive behavior in your child's list. What were the consequences of each action? Speculate about what would have happened if he had acted more prudently. Expand your list to look like the one in Figure 9.2. The purpose of this exercise is to ensure that your child understands that impulsiveness is related not only to acting quickly but also to acting without thinking first. Carl and his mom discussed the possible consequences of running into the street, leaving his homework and books at home and blurting out answers in class. When Carl's mom asked him what happened when he left his work and books at home, he said he would have to redo the work at school. It quickly became clear to Carl that taking a few moments to think before acting could save him effort and perhaps injury.

IMPULSIVE ACTS	THOUGHT-OUT ACTS
Running into the street.	Pausing at light or curb and looking both ways.
Leaving house without schoolbooks.	Putting books in bookbag when homework is done.
Interrupting conversations.	Saying, "Excuse me, " and waiting to speak.
Grabbing toy from little brother.	Asking to play with toy.
Pushing in line.	Waiting for a turn.

FIGURE 9.1

Impulsive versus Planned Acts

Prioritize the situations in which your child acts impulsively.
Once your child grasps the concept of what impulsive behavior
is and understands its negative consequences, you are ready to
pinpoint those aspects of his behavior you want to focus on
changing. Review your lists as well as recent experiences. How
does he act impulsively? In what situations? When? Using a
form like the one shown in Figure 9.3, rank-order the situations
in terms of which ones you want to work on first. It will be
easier if initial selections are those that you have more control
over rather than those where there are many circumstances
beyond your control. If there is a situation that may endanger
your child, that is a good reason to address it early.

Teach a hesitation response. To be able to think before acting, your child is going to have to lengthen the time between
impulse and action. To do that he's going to have to learn to
hesitate between thought and deed.

Impulsive Acts	Negative Consequences	Alternative If Thought
Left homework at home.	Redo work.	Free time at school.
Running into street.	Hit by car.	Safe crossing.
Blurting out	Not called on/ reprimanded.	Answer question/ good grade.
Grabbing toy.	Lose toy.	Play with toy.

FIGURE 9.2

Impulsive Acts and Consequences

Beginning with the first situation on your list, simulate the natural circumstances as closely as possible. If you are working on pausing before your child crosses the street, then go to the road's edge. Demonstrate how you want your child to hesitate, look both ways to be sure the road is clear, and then cross. Have him practice the response a number of times under your direct supervision before he tries it on his own. Be sure to give him

I AM IMPULSIVE

1._____

2._____

3._____

4._____

5._____

6._____

7._____

8._____

9._____

10._____

FIGURE 9.3
"I Am Impulsive" List

lots of praise and specific feedback on what he is doing right, as Carl's mother did when she said, "When I see you stop a foot away from the curb, then I know you're really thinking. You looked both ways two times!"

Each situation on your list is likely to require a different hesitation response. Before leaving the house, your child may need to stop, take one step backwards and check himself from head to toes to see if he has left anything behind. Be sure he actually goes through the motions of patting his coat, pockets, and so forth.

In certain situations just pausing and counting softly as he scans the room or reviews the activity will be all that is needed. Checkers is a great game for testing this new skill. For some children the desire to make a move on the board is as strong an impulse as any. Learning to monitor the moves pays off in a better game. Even when the child is convinced he knows what

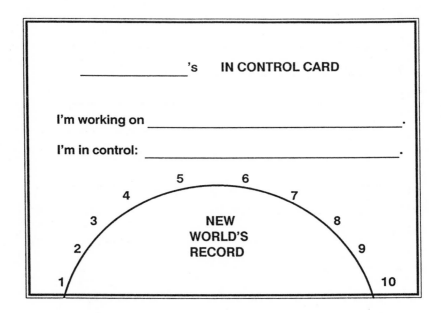

FIGURE 9.4
"I'm in Control" Card

move to make, he should be encouraged to pause and count to himself while he peruses the board one more time.

Specify controlled responding. Work on one target behavior at a time, together specifying exactly what the controlled response to that impulsive behavior should be. Copy the "I'm in Control" Card in Figure 9.4. Define the behavior and the controlled response you will be looking to reinforce. On Carl's card in Figure 9.5 the behavior is "crossing the street" and the controlled response is pausing at the curb and looking both ways. You can also see that the number of occasions when Carl practiced this behavior is tallied on the card. He's going for a new world's record of six times in a row!

Give massed practice. In order to help your child learn this new type of responding, he needs many opportunities in a row to practice it. Rehearsal is crucial. If you are working on crossing the street, you cannot wait for an occasion to arise when he

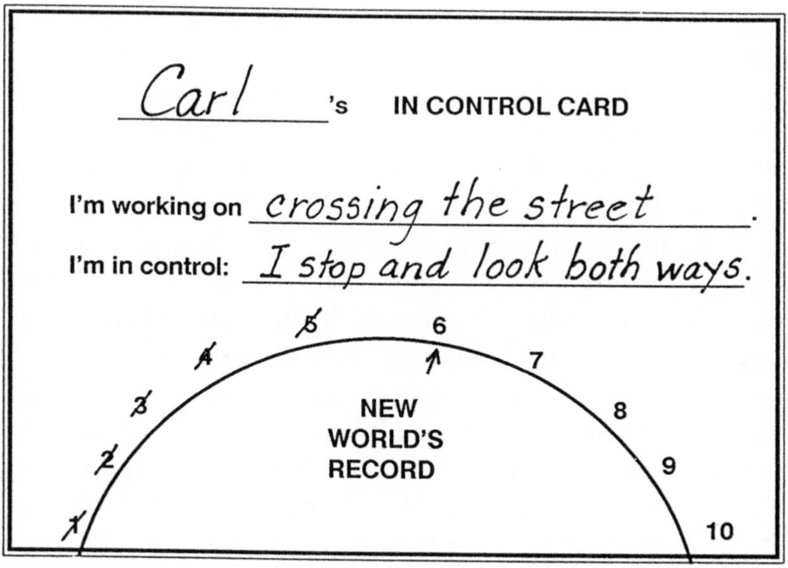

FIGURE 9.5
Carl's "I'm in Control" Card

needs to cross the street. Work with him for twenty minutes at a time, repeatedly practicing the correct response under your supervision. It is fine to make it as much fun as you can, but as with any new skill, it takes practice to achieve mastery. Similarly, concentration on teaching your child to take turns while playing games might dictate that you set up checkers tournaments or marathon card games, so the hesitation response becomes ingrained.

Reinforce nonimpulsive responding. Each time you observe the child using his hesitation response, praise him. You will have to judge what kind of praise is most appropriate for your youngster. For the older or more self-conscious child, a prearranged signal or whispered comment may be more effective than any elaborate remarks. Of course if your child enjoys public praise, then feel free to pile it on.

Quite likely you will need to use additional reinforcement to get this new behavior going. Use the reward system described in Chapter 3, awarding one point each time your child uses his new skills to act cautiously. In addition, when he sets a new record, award a bonus of ten points. Remember, it is important to permit him to trade in his points and earn rewards in a timely manner.

Use positive practice and overcorrection when impulsiveness occurs. No matter how much you praise and reinforce your child, he will undoubtedly act impulsively at times. To speed the learning process, you must correct impulsive behavior when it occurs. Rather than falling into that old criticism trap, try employing overcorrection and positive-practice techniques. When your child fails to hesitate before acting, explain that he must need more practice in hesitating. Assure him you are not angry but that it is your responsiblity as a parent to help him practice this new response until it becomes habit. Rehearse the hesitation response for the situation several times in a row. If he impulsively interrupts a conversation without saying, "Excuse me," and waiting for acknowledgment, have him walk out of the room, return, wait for a gap in the conversation, say, "Excuse me," pause for your okay and then make his comment. When you utilize this technique, repeat the desired action at least five times. For other impulsive acts, such as rushing through a homework assignment, copying the page two times may be sufficient. On the other hand, running through the living room and over the furniture might require ten practices. You may find it necessary to guide the younger, more resistant child through these practices manually. The older child needs to understand that his privileges rest on his compliance during the practice period. At the end of the session, lightly remind your child you are always available for extra practice any time he needs it.

FIGURE 9.6
"I Can Control Myself" List

Give recognition for mastery of each situation. When a child masters self-control in a particular situation for several weeks, add this feat to an "I Can Control Myself" List copied from the one in Figure 9.6. Whenever a new behavior is added to the list, your child should be able to choose one major item from a menu of choices you have provided. Instructions and suggestions for how to create this menu are discussed in Chapter 3. Review this control list regularly to solidify his success. If he begins to lose ground in a particular area, inquire whether he thinks he can still control this type of impulsiveness. How? Role-play for a little while, until he begins to feel comfortable with his ability. Avoid criticism. Provide extra practice and praise his perseverance. If the skill should need to be temporarily removed from the list, assure him it will be replaced as soon as he renews control.

10

■

Beating Distractions

A jet roars over the school. Some students take no notice of it, while others glance toward the sky and then return to work. One second grader, Greg, turns to the window, catches sight of the plane, locks onto it, tracking it first by sight and then sound. Long after it is past the playground—in fact, until his teacher calls his name—Greg continues daydreaming about being a pilot.

Greg is also distracted by items less exotic than flying machines. The air conditioner running, other kids whispering, pictures pinned to the bulletin board, words penciled into his desk by previous students—all these vie for his attention. A picture of Mount Everest in his social studies text reminds him of the time his family went skiing. Within moments his mind is jumping from downhill racing to throwing snowballs, from Frosty the Snowman to the holiday gifts he received last December. Quite a whirlwind of imaginative events, but all in a day's thoughts for some ADHD children.

A million distractions lurk to draw the attention of the ADHD youngster away from a task. Walking upstairs to retrieve a coat requires the concentration of a dodgeball survivor to ignore the obstacles that block the path. Distractibility, not poor memory, makes these children seem like little absentminded professors.

Take a second to imagine what it is like to be attracted by every stimulus. If you have had any interruptions as you read this page, you know that even one hitch breaks the line of thought so you must reread the page to comprehend the meaning. Without the ability to filter out extraneous sights and sounds, concentrating on simple directions is like trying to do your tax return in the middle of Grand Central Station. You feel as if you are treading water. True, you stay afloat, but it is hard to get anywhere. Such is the impasse of the ADHD youngster, who is always in the middle of a task, often behind and rarely able to complete it.

Teaching the ADHD youngster to ignore distractions is not an impossible task, but it does take time. Before shutting them out, the ADHD youngster must learn to identify his distractions, then purposefully block them and, finally, internalize some filtering strategies so the distractions lose their attraction. Keeping in mind that this is a long-term goal—one you will repeatedly return to over the years—use the following steps to help your child become less distractible.

Make a list of distractions. What seems to distract your child the most? Some children are most distracted by visual stimuli; others by the sounds they hear. Still others are diverted by both external and internal distractions, such as thoughts, feelings, the gurgling of food digesting or other physical sensations. In order to beat distractions, your child must first gain awareness of them.

▪ Become aware of distractions. Together, like two detectives working on a case, accumulate a list of distractions that pull your child away from a task. The more you gather, the clearer everyone will become about what distracts your child. Include in your tally where a particular annoyance occurred and what your child was doing at the time. When beginning the inventory, suggest one distraction, then elicit others from your child. During the next few days and weeks you both will add to the list as others become apparent. When your child gets sidetracked, inquire about what got him that time. The example in Figure 10.1 suggests how the exercise might look. Working on written work at school, Mal was distracted by other students talking. When he read silently or had a chore to do, the way he felt or things he thought about interfered. Greg told his dad that when he did his homework, he was distracted by the model airplane hanging in his room. After you have developed a fairly extensive list of situations and distractions, review it together. Which categories have the most distractions? Which type of distraction catches your child's attention most often? Is there a category of distractions that your child finds easier to ignore than others? Similarly, are there situations in which he is clearly more distractible?

▪ Record the strength of the distractions. The information you have collected in the survey of distractions will help your child understand what diverts him. Now apply this information to the Distract-o-Meters pictured in Figure 10.2. Using a copy of the meters, evaluate your child's distractibility in each area. How much is your son attracted by visual stimuli? A lot or a little? Does your daughter find it impossible to resist noises? Now, draw an arrow on the Distract-o-Meter to indicate how easily your child can *ignore* each type of distraction.

In the example, Greg and his parents rated his ability to ignore visual distractions and auditory distractions as poor, but he was less distracted by internal cues so they rated that area fair. The Distract-o-Meter also provides a way to mark progress. Date each marking on the dial, then as your child's ability to disregard distractions improves, a new needle can be drawn to record it.

Teach your child how to use a distraction zapper. With the identification of what distracts your child, your initial detective work is complete. The team is ready to work on ignoring distractions. Obviously it will be easier for you to manipulate the external environment than your child's internal one, so training begins with visual and auditory distractions. Later, we focus on runaway thoughts and internal stimuli that lead to daydreaming and hinder progress.

Situation or Task	Distractions		
	Auditory	Visual	Internal
Doing written seatwork at school.	Students talking.		
Reading a book.			Thinking about what I was doing after school.
Doing homework.		Looking at model airplane hanging from ceiling.	
Putting bookbag away after school.			Smells from the kitchen made my stomach growl, thought about great desserts and forgot bookbag.

WHAT ARE MY DISTRACTIONS?

FIGURE 10.1

Greg's List of Distractions

You know yourself you cannot just tell your child to disregard distractions. He has heard that repeatedly for years, and it has not worked. Children need a way to externalize the process, so they can become aware of it before assuming active control over attending. As a rule of thumb, if you make it fun for children, you are halfway to the goal. To accomplish both purposes, we use a technique we've labeled distraction zapping. Kids love it and it is easy to teach.

Younger children, especially boys, prize action-oriented zappers. Nine-year-old Chris decided his defense against distracters would be a make-believe ray gun. As he climbed upstairs to get his jacket, he pointed his finger at the plastic figure laying on the bottom landing, zapped it out of his mind and proceeded up the steps. As he walked down the hall, he eradicated a warehouse of diversions that would have garnered his attention previously. Now it is true that he zapped his little brother, but he

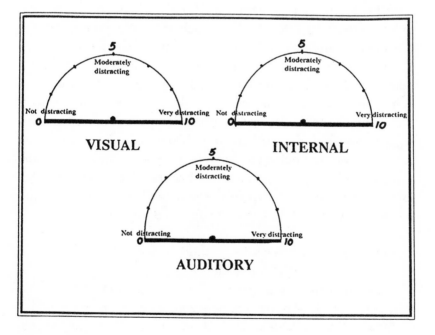

FIGURE 10.2
Distract-o-Meters

did not grab him, which would also have happened a day earlier. So this was progress.

On his way to his room, Chris zapped eight items but returned with his jacket in a reasonable amount of time. His mom praised him for running the course in record time without getting sidetracked. Other youngsters have devised different zappers. From Superman's breath, which blows the distractions away, to Jeannie's blink, the key is to find one that appeals to your child and is age-appropriate. The older the child, the more subtle or cool the gesture must be.

As you read about the distraction-zapping technique, you may fear that you are creating additional problems with this zapper. Our experience proves otherwise. As your child's skills become more sophisticated, his zapping will become more refined. Naturally, or with a few suggestions, he will tone down the gesture so it is less noticeable. Within a few weeks, Chris shifted from full-photo phasers with sound effects to a silent push-button phaser shot from the hip. Gradually he progressed to forms used by older children, such as blinking away distractions and finally just giving the annoyance the evil eye.

• Discuss potential zappers with your youngsters. Make it a question of you and your child against the problem. "I want to help you find a way to stay on task. We know your mind is pulled by the television set, noises in the hall, the bird outside the window and many other things. Do you think we can create some motion that helps you 'disintegrate' the distraction so you can get back on task—some kind of zapper?" He can create his own zapper or suggest one from the list below. Have your child try out a few. It will be fun and you can do it too.

1. Phaser Gun: The classic pretend gun children have acted shoot-'em-up with for decades.
2. Superman Breath: As Superman blows criminals out of this world, the child blows the distraction out of his path.
3. Magic Blink: Like a wizard, children enjoy blinking the distraction out of sight and mind.
4. Evil Eye: Basically this is a dirty look directed toward the offending distracter.

5. Magic Wand: With the stroke of his magic wand, your child may enjoy having the power to make distractions disappear.
6. Finger Snap: If she has the beat, then that finger-snapping, toe-tapping sound may snap her distractions away.
7. Finger Point: Miss Manners may say pointing is not polite, but if it works for your child, we will not mind and neither will you.

As you may have guessed, this list is the work of some creative young minds. Given the opportunity, your child will devise a clever way to zap those distractions or, perhaps, simply turning his back on the intrusion is the distraction fighter for your child. Whatever works for your child should be encouraged.

Teach your child to zap distractions at play. Now it is time to put the zapper to work.

• Create a situation with numerous distractions that your child can easily zap and ignore. An activity that your child enjoys and is usually able to complete, such as playing with a favorite toy, makes a good starting point. Explain that the goal of the game is for you to try to draw his interest away from the toy, but that his job is to focus his attention on the toy. He can earn points for zapping the distractions you send his way. Take several moments to practice, showing him how to zap the distracter with barely a glance in its direction.

• Entice your child with several distracters from the distracter list you compiled previously. Initially use those distracters that were rated as less intense. At this point do not worry too much if your child is easily excited, tending to get carried away with zapping. This is normal and often occurs in the early stages of training. In fact you should view this as a motivating force that can be channeled into positive motivation. Praise your child for eradicating the distractions and returning to the toy quickly. You may discover it helps your child maintain his attention if he actually turns his entire body away from the distraction after it is zapped. Some children also like to say something like "Out of sight, out of mind," as they zap the offending interrupter.

• Add a point system to the training sessions. As discussed in

Chapter 3, allow your child to earn points for zapping offending distractions. Improvements in overall performance should also earn points. After every few training sessions check the Distract-o-meters with your child. Mark and date new lines to indicate how well he is able to resist each type of distraction. Even though you have not worked on internal distractions, allow the child to rate how well he resisted this type of interference. Any increases in the ability to resist distractions that you both agree on earn a point.

▪ Replay the training sessions every few days until your child can easily zap your interference and remain focused on his activity of choice. Do not become disheartened if progress is not rapid. Some children take longer to catch on; others resist the process. Keep the sessions brief and eventually your child will get the knack of it.

Zap getting sidetracked during less interesting tasks. Once your child can withstand being distracted from something he likes to do, he is ready for a bigger challenge—maintaining concentration during activities that are less amusing.

▪ Select a task from which he is easily distracted. No doubt something comes immediately to mind. If not, your list of distracters and situations is an excellent source for this information. If your child usually gets sidetracked when he is sent on an errand, design a mission that routes him past obvious distracters like the TV, toys, a radio, siblings or the family pet. He should be using the zapper quite naturally by now, but make sure it is in working order with a short refresher course before you begin.

▪ Set a reasonable time goal for accomplishing the task. As he pursues the goal, time how long it actually takes him to report back with evidence the job is complete. Give your child feedback on how long it actually took him to accomplish the task and praise him for approaching, meeting, or beating his time goal. Your child should earn one point for getting close to the time, two points for making it and three points if he beats the time.

▪ Debriefing after training sessions is important. Provide an opportunity for your child to relate how he used his zapper.

Always praise his progress and, in the initial stages of training, award one point each time he uses his zapper appropriately. Whenever he sets out on a mission, set a reasonable time goal, then reward him according to the same formula.

- Use consequences to remove hindrances to progress. If your child should get sidetracked occasionally, and most children do, determine what is distracting him. If an object or toy is the offender, put it in a time-out box, a box or container placed off-limits for a few days, so it will not interrupt him the next time. Should your child protest, calmly instruct him not to worry; there will be plenty of chances to prove it won't distract him again. If need be, show *your* ability to resist distractions by ignoring his indignation and turning attention to a new task.

- Record accomplishments. Any time your child completes an objective, record and praise it in a Zapper Log similar to the one shown in Figure 10.3. Like a running commentary on a child's progress, the Zapper Log is a permanent success record. Entries that would be appropriate for Chris's log would be "job: getting dressed for school" and "distraction zapped: zapped new toy in closet, didn't play with it, and made it to breakfast on time." In your child's log, you would also record the date and the number of points earned. Again, as before, every few days review the Distract-o-meters to mark progress.

Focus your attention on academic tasks. With the zapper working effectively during play and for simple tasks, you are both ready to turn your efforts toward academics.

Review your initial list of distractions to remind yourselves of the types of distracters that conflict with your child's concentration during academic pursuits. As you analyze the list, two questions are important to keep in mind.

What distracts your child in the classroom?
From which kinds of academic activities is he most easily distracted?

Pinpoint as best you can those distracters that prevent him from completing his work. Now that you are familiar with zapping, you will be able to suggest potential problems that impede progress.

▪ Select an initial task. Begin with any school assignment that is not difficult for your child, but is one from which his mind easily wanders. It might be math problems, reading passages or handwriting exercises. If your child is in preschool, then basic tasks like coloring, copying or listening to a story are also appropriate.

DAY	JOB	DISTRACTION ZAPPED	POINTS

ZAPPER LOG

FIGURE 10.3

Zapper Log

▪ Designate a training location where you can control the number of distractions. It could be a quiet corner or a room with few windows and knickknacks. As your child begins working on the task, present a distracter your child can fairly easily ignore. With Chris, one of the greatest difficulties in school was completing his math worksheets. This was chosen as his starting task. He was given a page of simple math problems. As he solved them, his mom slowly began to whisper to herself about chores she needed to do. Of no immediate interest to Chris, the mumbling was a background distraction that he was easily able to blink away and continue computing.

Each time Chris overlooked or zapped the whispers, he was quietly awarded a point. It was evident that Chris was succeeding in resisting the distraction because he did not look up from his paper and he maintained a consistent work rate before and after the attempted interruptions.

▪ Keep track of your child's progress on a personal progress card. Since much of the training will occur over a long period of time, it is important to maintain a record of your child's performance—as a reminder and a way of reinforcing improvement. Chris's card shown in Figure 10.4 indicates he completed seven math problems in four minutes and forty-eight seconds, zapped two distractions and kept right on working. By keeping the tasks fairly equal your child will recognize improvements in performance.

After each progress session, review your child's performance, prompting comments about how he was able to achieve this. Chris told his mom each time she whispered that he would silently repeat the problem "more loudly in his head" to block out her voice. Chris's mother marveled at his strategy and praised him for his ingenuity.

▪ Gradually increase both the intensity and the volume of the distracter. Based on what she felt her son would be able to handle, Chris's mom whispered louder and more often, occasionally including topics that might actually interest her son. All of this occurred over a period of months. At various times in the training, Chris and his mom decided to return to an easier level of distractions because he said, "It's too much for me."

After holding at this point for several weeks, he then was able to progress again. Eventually Chris was able to ignore his mom even when she acted like one of his school friends, taunting him with, "Hey Chris, did you see the basketball game last night?" Chris earned a well-deserved two points for not looking up or

MY PERSONAL RECORD				
Date	Task	# of Distractors	Time	Points
12/3	7 addition problems	2 whispers	4" 43'	2

FIGURE 10.4
Chris's Personal Record

stopping to respond to those kinds of comments. Chris's mom used other training ploys, like walking by, thumbing through a sports magazine and turning on the television set in the next room to lure his attention. Chris told us he would say to himself, "I can look at those later," and then silently verbalize what he was working on to maintain his concentration.

• Use audio and videotapes as distracters. You can tape auditory distractions, such as typical household noises, for your child to play as he works. You can also record songs or television shows. Play them at a volume so low initially that your child would have to strain to decipher the words. As he progresses, gradually increase the volume.

To use a video image to simulate visual distractions, begin by seating your child with his back to a television with the sound barely audible. It generally takes a long time for even a motivated child to learn to ignore visual distractions, so proceed very slowly, practicing once a week over many months. Always ask your child how he is able to pull off such a miracle as ignoring the television, and heap extra praise and points for effort and creativeness. It is not an impossible feat. We have seen children who could not ignore a TV playing in the downstairs den as they studied upstairs learn to ignore a set in the next room.

• Don't expect perfection. All of us are occasionally diverted and at times more distractible than on other occasions. This is certainly true of ADHD children. After working through distraction training, most children are very proud of themselves. A by-product of this experience seems to be that these children finally accept the fact that if they can ignore their favorite adventure show, they can certainly disregard the sound of the heat as it switches on. Children who accomplish this are very proud of their ability, although they may not always use it.

From time to time have your child rerate his distractibility and review the coping skills he has gained to maintain his motivation. Frequently praise him as you see the skill employed and occasionally surprise your child with a reward for using his new skills in a natural setting.

11
■

Stretching Attention Span

*W*hile hyperactivity may be the most conspicuous aspect of ADHD, in the long run, a short attention span hampers the ADHD youngster most. From keeping his eyes on the ball or her mind on the conversation to completing a school task, an individual is handicapped daily by attentional deficits. For many youngsters, the fact that disabilities from attention weaknesses persist long after hyperactivity diminishes is a major reason that any treatment for ADHD must emphasize the attentional aspects of the disorder.

While other parents may occasionally remind their child to pay attention to what is going on, each part of the day with an ADHD child is complicated by his vanishing concentration. Getting dressed in the morning, eating, following directions and executing school tasks take longer or never get done at all because the child is unable to maintain attention. Lengthening attention span is crucial to your child's success.

How do you do this? *One minute at a time.* Controlling activity level and impulsivity (Chapters 7 and 9), learning to relax (Chapter 8), and ignoring distractions (Chapter 10) all contribute to a longer attention span, but to get real improvement you must give direct instruction.

To begin, you cannot assume anything. Does your child understand what you mean when you say, "Pay attention"? We use the phrase so easily, but what does it imply? Take a moment to reread the first two paragraphs of this chapter. Pay attention to each sentence as you read.

What did you do as you read? Can you identify the process? Certainly you focused your eyes on the words in front of you, but more than likely you looked at whole words or even chunks of sentences as your eyes skimmed the lines, maybe the page. You know you were concentrating on the page, but it is hard to describe, isn't it? More than staring at the ink marks, you tried to reconstruct the meaning intended. Paying attention is so evident when you are doing it and so elusive if you are not.

In this chapter we present the steps you can follow to help your child lengthen his attention span.

Demonstrate paying attention to your child. Adults often refer to paying attention and attention span as if the concepts are automatically understood. By the time your child is five or six, he can begin to understand these concepts if they are explained clearly.

• Make the definition situational rather than general. Select an activity that your child enjoys and is related to the type of tasks he will be expected to engage in at school. Listening to a story is one that works well for many children. Talk to your child about what it means to attend to a story read aloud. In this case, it means looking at the book—the pictures and the print—and listening to the story so that the listener can relate it to someone else or answer questions about it.

Reminding your child that the goal in Beat the Clock was to

prevent his body from moving and wandering away, tell him that the task in this game is slightly more demanding. Now he must keep his body and mind in one place.

▪ Model key elements in paying attention for your child. Have your spouse or friend read a brief story to you or use a tape-recorded story. Instruct your child to watch as you listen because you will be paying attention to the story. Begin by looking at the reader (recorder) and listening closely for a minute, then pause to ask your child to evaluate how well you're paying attention. If he replies, "Well," ask how he could tell. You may need to offer hints such as, "What did I do with my eyes?" Then answer a few questions about the story to confirm your comprehension.

Continue the story but after ten seconds rap your fingers, look away a bit or make a few noises to suggest that your attention is waning. Again ask your child to rate you on paying attention. What did he notice this time? Together, list all of the things you did that showed him you were not paying attention. Suggest that your child or the reader ask you a few questions about the content. Answer incompletely so that it is apparent you missed parts of the story.

Continue to model paying attention, having your child observe and rate your performance at the end of each page. Praise him for correctly identifying what you did well and give him feedback on the signs he missed such as, "Yes, I followed the sentences with my eyes most of the time, but I started playing with my belt."

▪ Play the daydreaming game. Add a new element to your behavior. Many times individuals appear to be concentrating when they are really daydreaming. Demonstrate this aspect of inattention by reading to yourself as the reader or tape reads the same story aloud. After your child rates your performance, tell him that although you appeared to be paying attention, you were actually daydreaming about what you were going to have for dessert. Recommend that he watch the movement of your eyes, trying to detect when they stop moving across the print or the fact that you turned the page a little late. Now he will really have to be a detective to discover if you are attending. Informally keep score of how many times he recognizes inattention, always giving verbal feedback on what is really going on.

• Reverse roles, letting your child practice paying attention. If your child has difficulty, make a card that defines the important behaviors for paying attention. As shown in Figure 11.1, use symbols for children who cannot read all of the words, such as an "eye" for keeping his eyes on the page, "?" for answering questions and "open book" for turning the pages.

With the more able reader and the older child, substitute reading silently from a school text or library book for reading a story aloud. In the beginning, ask a few questions at the end of each paragraph or two. Begin slowly, having your child observe you until you believe he understands the concepts. He can score

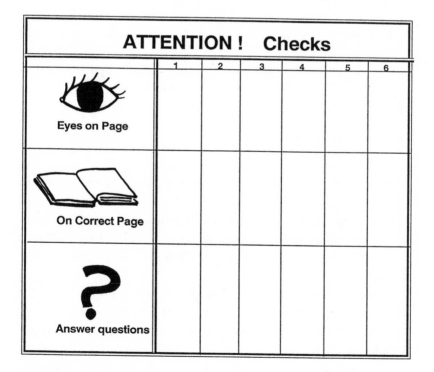

FIGURE 11.1
Hints for Paying Attention

your skills first, then change roles. Remember to praise him for doing a good job.

- Have random attention checks. Depending on the amount of text on the page, stop your child several times per page and then less frequently, so he never knows when to expect a check to occur. At each breaking point, ask him to rate his own behavior before sharing your observations. Acknowledge what he does right and, recognizing the inherent difficulty, be encouraging when he gets off task. Remind him that like any new skill, the attention game requires practice.

Teach your child to measure his span of attention. Once your child fully understands what you mean by paying attention, he is ready to measure his attention span. If your child is too young to tell time, timing will be your job. To help visualize an abstract concept, make an Attention Span Tape like the one illustrated in Figure 11.2. Although an older child will enjoy using the tape to demonstrate how long his attention span becomes, he will probably prefer controlling the stopwatch as he did with Statue.

- Review the rules for the attention game. Copy the "I Can Pay Attention" Card in Figure 11.3. Help your child fill in the formula:

I can pay attention to (task) .
My goal is to be able to do this for ＿＿ seconds/＿＿ minutes.

If your child is too young to do the recording, you will have to write the rules and review them aloud many times before beginning the game. To prompt attending, provide pictorial representations of the rules, such as the ones found in Figure 11.1 or actual photographs of your own childhood modeling attending behaviors.

- Time how long your child is able to stay on task. Begin the game. As long as your child shows all the overt signs of attending, continue the timer, unless he volunteers that his mind has wandered. If he reports that his mind has strayed, stop the watch and praise him for attending for ＿＿ seconds/minutes as well as being aware of when his mind wandered. If you catch him, praise his accomplishment no matter how small and re-

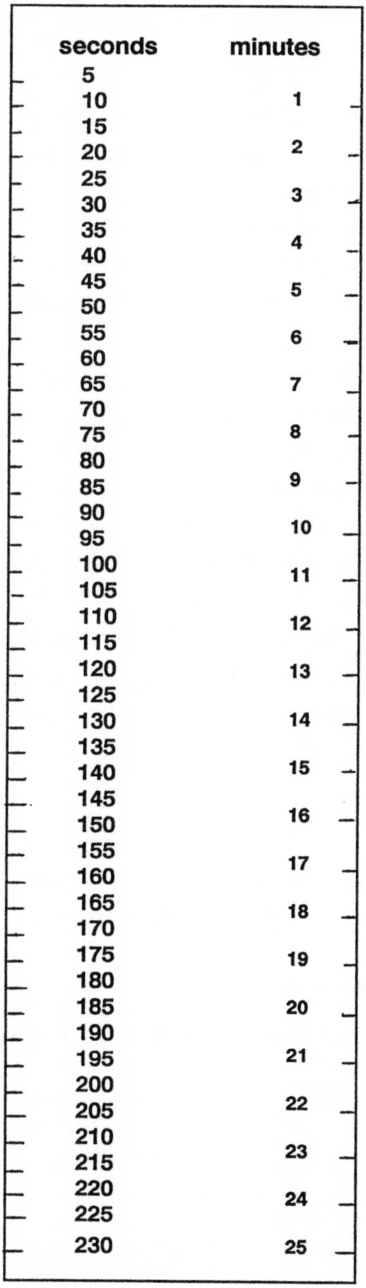

seconds	minutes
5	
10	1
15	
20	2
25	
30	3
35	
40	4
45	5
50	
55	6
60	
65	7
70	
75	8
80	
85	9
90	
95	10
100	
105	11
110	12
115	
120	13
125	
130	14
135	
140	15
145	
150	16
155	
160	17
165	18
170	
175	19
180	
185	20
190	
195	21
200	
205	22
210	
215	23
220	24
225	
230	25

FIGURE 11.2

Attention Span Tape

view what he did correctly. Invite him to guess how you knew his concentration was broken. If he identifies the telltale signs, applaud his awareness. If not, identify the behaviors that alerted you. Ignore any arguing, should it occur, by telling your child he has many other chances and restart the game.

• Record increasing span of concentration with the attention tape. As shown in Figure 11.4, with Jan's attention span tape, your child can keep his own record by marking the tape with a colored star or small sticker, the date, and trial number at the point that indicates the number of seconds or minutes he attended. As with Statue and Beat the Clock your child earns one point for matching a previous record and two points for breaking it. Matched or broken records should be the only ones marked on the tape.

During the first session, play the game several times in a row. Afterwards, practice the game every few days until your youngster gets a clear notion of how long he is able to pay attention

---

I CAN PAY ATTENTION!

I can pay attention to _____(task).

My goal is to be able to do this for _____minutes_____ seconds.

To do this I must:

1._____

2._____

3._____

4._____

5._____

FIGURE 11.3
"I Can Pay Attention" Card

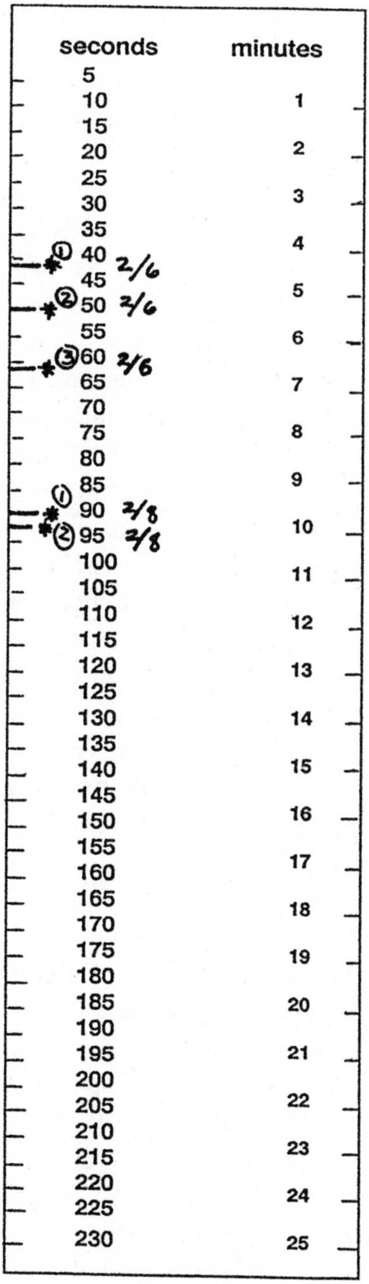

FIGURE 11.4

Jan's Attention Span Tape

to this particular type of task. Do not overdo the exercise to the point the child feels stressed or pushed.

Stretch attention span. When your child has a basic understanding of how long he can pay attention to a listening task like the one used in the training sessions, you are ready to work toward increasing his span of attention for other tasks.

▪ Select a target task. Begin with a simple task but one your child has difficulty completing because he does not concentrate. For example, Jerilyn was a whiz in math. She rarely computed incorrectly, but she could not keep her mind on the task. When Jerilyn's parents began attention training, they used math problems because the skill would not complicate the instruction. Social studies, math or any other content area that has inherent difficulty will not be a good choice. For some children, it may be necessary to get some additional help with reading or other basic skills before attention training will be beneficial.

▪ Measure his attention span for the target. Using a new attention span tape, play the attention game several times until you have a feel for how long he is able to attend to the task generally. As before, identify signs of attention and distraction, freely giving your positive feedback and checking on his perceptions. During this preliminary period, award one point per trial. Record his times on the tape and on a summary chart like the one in Figure 11.5. Calculate his average time and also circle his shortest and longest times for the day.

Set a goal. After reviewing his times, define a realistic goal and ask your child to mark it on the attention tape. It is helpful if you operationalize the goal for the child. For example, if reading for one minute is the first goal, help him to estimate how many pages that might be. If the task is math, how many problems does he think he might complete during the allotted time? Encourage him to set attainable goals that will permit him to increase the time he concentrates on his work.

Begin practice sessions. Effective use of this technique requires your immediate feedback. You cannot expect your child to take responsibility for his own learning yet. Your child will progress most quickly if you observe him working and give him steady feedback just as you did in the training sessions.

• Together decide on one time each day to practice. Assuming the goal is less than five minutes initially, practice time will be a five- or ten-minute period rather than his entire homework session.

• Minimize distractions. For the training, prepare a clear work space in a quiet room that has few visual distractions.

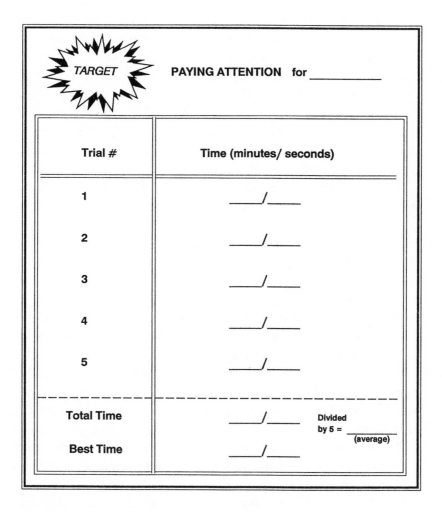

FIGURE 11.5
Summary Chart

Do not forget to inform other family members not to disturb you.

• Time and record each trial. When the child is ready, start the timer and continue until your child shows indications he is off task. As before, one point is earned for matching his longest previous record, two points for a new record. While perfect comprehension or workmanship is not the immediate concern, take a brief glance over his work or ask a few questions to validate his attention. Whenever he loses his focus short of his goal, reassure him that he has many more chances.

• Use attention checks to boost his attending time. Sometimes children will initially do very well, but find it difficult to maintain or get beyond a particular level of attention. Set a timer for varying times within that period. For example, perhaps your child has concentrated for several five-minute periods in a row, yet found it difficult to maintain that. Tell him you are going to set a timer for attention checks during his next trial session. Repeatedly set the timer for varying time intervals within the five-minute period—perhaps thirty seconds, then one minute forty-five seconds, then one and a half minutes. Tell your child that when the bell rings he is immediately to circle the spot where he is working and then continue. Your goal with this technique is to prompt further attention, not interrupt the task. If he surpasses his five-minute goal, signal the success as you normally would. Continue the random checks until he finally loses concentration. In this case, he would earn an additional two points for breaking his record and mark this achievement on the attention span tape.

Slowly lengthen the intermittent time intervals so your child is working for longer periods toward the goal. Eventually he should be able to work for increasingly longer periods without interruption.

Let the child practice on his own. As your child progresses, gradually eliminate your supervision. In essence you will become an intermittent reinforcer yourself, going and coming while your child continues working. Leave the room; if your child is on task when you return, he earns a point.

• Teach your child to record his own times. At stage two,

allow your child to practice setting the timer and recording the times himself. If he needs occasional reminders to attend, make a tape recording of the timer/beeper ringing at random intervals that you prerecord. For some children the tape itself may be distracting while others accumulate additional time because of the recorded prompts.

• Reward your child for accurate recording. When your child records his own points, check his totals with yours. To encourage accuracy, agreement should earn a bonus point. Close each session by reviewing the attention span tape and setting goals for the next trial.

Phase out your supervision naturally by allowing your child to assume more responsibility. Let him work alone for part of each session; come in only every so often to see if he is on task. He may reward himself with an extra point if he is on task as you come in the room.

If you can see the product of his work in terms of pages read or problems completed, then validate the record and award points. Give him the benefit of the doubt unless there is an obvious discrepancy. Review and initial his attention span tape, recognizing progress.

Over time your child's ability to work alone on the target task should increase. If problems reoccur, then augment his learning with some supervised practice sessions.

Select a new target behavior. It would be nice if this exercise automatically led to increased attention span for all types of needed tasks. Unfortunately this rarely happens with ADHD children. You will have to target new behaviors and repeat these steps. It probably feels as if this is going to take forever. It will take a long time, but remember you are helping your child to develop lifelong skills.

Continue to review the progress your child has already made and the benefits of training. If he is able to concentrate and get his written work done in twenty minutes instead of one and a half hours, this automatically translates into extra playtime. Reviewing such facts helps keep up everyone's morale.

12

∎

Following
Rules

*I*f there is
one characteristic that causes more problems than any other for
the ADHD child, his parents and teachers, it is the inability to
follow rules. So universal is this conclusion that some leading
researchers have begun to label ADHD as a disorder of rule-
governed behavior. From darting into the street to not sitting
quietly in class, if it is a behavior that emanates from a generally known rule, the ADHD child typically violates it.

There are a number of reasons why ADHD children have difficulty following rules. Inattentiveness is the most obvious one.
The ADHD child does not comply with the rules because he is
unaware of them. As everyone else is listening to the teacher's
explanation, his mind is wandering. So absorbed by whatever

captures his attention, he can totally miss directions given, as well as the more subtle clues embedded in facial expression, tone of voice and those key words that usually prompt others. When you walk into a room, where do you look? More than likely you scan the environment, searching for anything that stands out in an effort to discover what rules are operating or how you should act. Most children gradually acquire an awareness of what is important and then attend to it. Streetwise, "teacherwise" and "parentwise," most children gradually develop a keen sixth sense of what is important to observe. To the ADHD child, everything is equally important. No one feature of his environment is automatically more demanding, so the ADHD child has difficulty knowing where to focus his attention.

The inability to attend selectively to the environment is very disruptive. While another child might walk into a classroom, immediately note all the students are sitting in their seats listening to the teacher at the front of the room and act accordingly, these conclusions can easily elude the ADHD child. Most of the time he does not know where to pinpoint his attention, but when he does focus well, it is usually not long enough to gain the crucial information. These weaknesses in selecting where to attend and in sustaining attention make it exceedingly difficult for many ADHD children to play by the rules.

Many ADHD youngsters have difficulty following directions casually called to a class, adhering to routines and adjusting to the unwritten customs that affect much of our behavior because the intricate social cues that others pick up totally escape them. Seven-year-old Allen constantly interrupted conversations. He could parrot rules about waiting to speak, but he always intruded midsentence because he was totally oblivious to normal pauses in speech. Forget asking most ADHD children to do something from another room. This definitely reduces the chances of response. Even good eye contact will not confirm the child is listening. Surely you can recall countless times when your child looked you in the eye and nodded as you spoke, but not one word registered.

Impulsiveness also plagues many of the actions of ADHD youngsters. Invariably parents must teach their children not to run into the street after a ball. Few boys and girls learn the lesson immediately, but after a few trials and their consequences, the rule is mastered. ADHD kids have particular difficulty with this rule and others that directly conflict with their impulsiveness. Running into the street, not interrupting, waiting, sharing and not blurting out the answers in class require some sublimation of desire. The child must inhibit his need to make the answer known, ask a question, get the ball or play with a toy. That is tough for most youngsters, but the reactions are so strong in the ADHD child, that the feat is similar to controlling a reflex.

Most rule-governed behaviors require some constriction of motion. As you can imagine, this presents an automatic conflict for the hyperactive child. To sit in a seat and not get up without permission demands some inhibition of movement. Here is a child whose legs are commonly in motion, swaying, rocking or kicking; he squirms a little and pretty soon either his feet have him walking or the chair is precariously balanced on its back legs. He never would anticipate that he might fall on his head.

Many problems ADHD children fall into stem from the fact they do not anticipate the consequences of their behavior. Afterwards, they seem to react differently to the consequences they encounter. They do not look ahead, but even when they run into a wall, they do not learn from it. They will run down the same hall and into the wall on another day.

Through the years psychologists and educators have repeatedly told parents and teachers about the importance of positive and negative consequences in teaching behavior. This is doubly true for ADHD children. As we discussed in Chapter 3, motivation, important to all children, is crucial for ADHD children. These youngsters require more reinforcement to learn a rule, extra motivation to maintain their behavior, and negative consequences to learn the effects of inappropriate behavior.

What this means for you and your ADHD youngster is that learning and maintaining rule-governed behavior will take time and effort. Quite likely that is more time and more effort than would be required for other children, but do not despair. The reinforcement system in Chapter 3 and the techniques in Chapters 7, 9 and 11 will help your child learn to control his activity level, impulses and attentional processes to the point that listening to instructions and following rules will be easier. It's a lot to learn but you won't do it all at once. In this chapter we will help you work on building your child's rule-governed behavior.

Add one rule at a time. You could probably list a number of rules your child is not following consistently. If you revved up to fix this pattern, your natural inclination might be to make a new list of the rules, print them bolder and post them again. If you have considered doing this, resist the urge!

Our experiences have taught us that parents and children are most successful when they work on one behavior at a time, and that's even more true when it comes to ADHD kids and rules. Select one rule, work on it until the child follows it consistently —not perfectly, but most of the time—then add another.

Where do you begin? Which rule should you select? The most important criterion is that you attempt to select a rule you believe your child can master fairly quickly.

Be specific. Most adults are too general when it comes to rules. We assume that if we tell a child generally what we want him to do, he will do it as specifically as we expect. Understandably this rarely happens. Again, it is even more difficult with an ADHD child. If you say, "Don't leave things lying around the house!" it is quite unlikely your child will place all her dirty clothes in the hamper, put her toys in the closet, and carry her dirty dishes to the sink. Not this year! You greatly increase the odds in your favor if you state one of these requests as descriptively as possible. Define the action specifically and positively: "Put your dirty clothes and towels in the hamper in your bathroom before coming downstairs."

An effective rule states the action in a positive way (Put), tells the child what, how and where (all the dirty clothes and towels in the hamper) and when it should be accomplished (before coming downstairs).

Use multiple prompts whenever possible. You do not want to have to constantly remind your child to follow a rule. Still, the ADHD youngster will need extra cues to help him remember.

Instead of involving yourself in an ongoing hassle, you and your child should devise ways to prompt his memory. A little environmental engineering can be very helpful and take some of the pressure off you.

One family we worked with devised an ingenious plan to help their son follow the rule about putting all his toys in a toy chest. They positioned the box in such a way that he had to walk around it to get to his bed. The child also made signs that he stuck on his doorknob, bathroom medicine cabinet and alarm clock that prodded him to follow the rule. Other parents and their youngsters have thought of interesting places to post notes so that the reminders are very hard to miss. Ten-year-old Mark placed a fairly large sign in his underwear drawer because he said he was sure he would have to open that drawer every day! One key to success, of course, is that the notes be mutually created and placed by parents and kids.

Use your imagination. All types of systems can work. Some families have set an extra alarm clock for the time of the chore. That worked so well reminding one young man to feed his pet that the dog learned to head for the bowl when he heard the alarm ring! Another child suggested that his parents clear their throats when he needed to remember a rule at meals.

Pick one rule and explore with your child ways in which elements in the environment can be manipulated to prompt his memory. Let him help you post notes, set alarm clocks, agree on hand signals and other ways of assisting him to follow the rule without your having to nag constantly. The more you can let something in the environment serve as the prompt, the better.

Provide immediate feedback. All of us desire feedback about how we are doing, but ADHD youngsters need more of it, more quickly, in order to be able to improve their behavior patterns. It is essential to give feedback as soon as your child has followed a rule. Likewise if he is about to break a rule or already has done so, he must know that.

Obviously, you want to avoid embarrassing or harassing your child with your feedback. Younger children are more receptive to direct feedback. When a young child follows a rule, most of the time you can openly praise the behavior. If your son sits quietly in his seat at the table with both feet on the floor, rather than saying, "Good boy," try, "You are doing a very good job of following the rule and sitting in your chair. Do you know you have not rocked once since we sat down for dinner!" Specific feedback clearly informs the child about the behavior you are praising.

When your child seems to need a hint or breaks a rule, restate the rule for him: "The rule is: We stay seated in our chairs with the legs of the chair on the floor."

You know your child better than anyone else, but older kids are more apt to react negatively to direct statements of praise or disapproval—at least in public. Instead, in advance, work out some kind of private signal that conveys your message, such as clearing your throat or tapping on the table, until your child catches your expression. Or at an opportune moment pull him aside and privately praise his rule-following or give feedback on a broken rule. Ideally you should tell the good or bad news as soon after the event as possible.

Use both positive and negative natural consequences. It would be nice if talk alone would motivate your child to follow rules, but you already know that words are probably not enough. In order to teach and maintain good rule-following you will have to use additional positive and negative consequences.

The best kinds of consequences are natural ones that are logically related to the behavior they follow. When your child picks up all his toys and puts them in the proper place, it is quite logical that this might allow him more time to play with a special toy that becomes available since the rest of the toys were put away so well. If, on the other hand, he fails to pick up his toys, then of course the special toy is unavailable. Furthermore, any toys that were not put away by the deadline are put into a time-out box, where they must be earned back one at a time by following the rules.

It is not always easy to think of an appropriate consequence, but with practice you will get the knack of it. The following ideas will assist you.

Ask yourself what would be a natural outcome if your child

did follow the rule. For example, if your child gets dressed quickly in the morning, then logically she will have extra time to do something she likes to do before the car pool arrives. In this case, you can think of many natural outcomes that are possibly reinforcing.

Since natural reinforcers are activities your child already likes to do, there are many ways to stack the odds in your favor. If your child loves watching television, riding his bike or playing a game with you, then those activities are naturally reinforcing to him. If you are working on a rule related to one of these activities, you can incorporate privileges related to these outcomes into your plan.

Ask yourself what damage is done by not following the rule. If your child is supposed to put his things away after using them and he leaves his bike in the driveway, then a natural outcome is that the bike is off-limits for a specified period of time. Any natural outcome that increases the likelihood the child will comply with a rule can be applied as a natural consequence.

Two particularly effective techniques that can enhance the effectiveness of natural consequences are called overcorrection and positive practice. These techniques not only teach the desired behavior but also teach the child that it is easier to comply with the rule the first time. For example, your son is learning the rule "Dirty clothes must be put into the clothes hamper." If he leaves his pajamas on the floor, you might assume he has not learned the rule because he has not had enough practice following the behavior. So it is your job to provide practice with overcorrection and positive practice. With tongue in cheek, present this in a positive way, claiming, "You know this is really my fault that you do not follow the hamper rule; I just have not provided enough practice." Then supervise him picking up the clothing left on the floor as well as any others left out elsewhere in the house ("Oh no, I bet you need some more practice"). Overcorrection comes into play as you search through the closet, under the bed and in other places that might have items out of place. If you cannot find any misplaced clothing, have him practice picking up the same piece of clothing from ten different places in the house where items have been left previously. If your child balks at the idea, manually guide him through the practices.

Use extra reinforcement and response cost. In addition to using natural consequences, extra reinforcement is extremely effective in initiating a new rule. As an extension of your natural consequences, it can provide a natural way to reinforce your child. Additionally if desired, you can strengthen your reinforcement with a reward system.

- Setting new records. Each time your child follows the rule keep a count of it. "Hey, that's really great! That's one more time you followed the rule." "Boy, that's two times in a row you followed this rule." Continue announcing each new record. When your child breaks the rule, tell him, "That's okay, you kept the rule three times in a row; let's see if you can go for a new world's record and make it four or more times in a row!"

A copy of the graph like the one in Figure 12.1 will help your child see his string of successes and keep track of his world records. Each time the rule is followed, color in a square on the graph. When it is broken, total the successes. If it represents a new world's record, place a star at the top of the row, reward your child as described below. If he did not set a new record, let him know he has another opportunity to break the record.

- Using a reward system. A token system like the one described in Chapter 3 can motivate your child to cooperate. First decide which type of system you will use. You may prefer a tangible token. In Chapter 3, we describe a paper-and-pencil system that also permits a child to see his points accumulate.

Tokens or checks should be earned in the following manner:

- Three tokens are earned for following a rule without any reminders. Two tokens are earned if he follows the rule with only one prompt and none if it takes more.
- If a child breaks a rule or ignores a prompt, then it costs him two tokens or checks.

Response cost, a very effective tool with the ADHD child, is an essential part of the reinforcement system, since it supplies the negative consequences for the child's actions. To maximize the effectiveness of your reinforcement keep these points in mind:

- Any reinforcement system should be applied to only one rule so as to maximize its effectiveness. The child should not be able to earn tokens for anything else during the time you are teaching him the rule.
- The items and privileges that are earned on the token menu are available only by earning them with tokens for rule-following. If a trip to your child's favorite ice cream parlor costs

FIGURE 12.1
Rule Success

five tokens, the child should not be able to supplement the cost of the trip with his own money.

- The payoff must be prompt. When you are teaching a rule, enlist the help of those who come in contact with your child. Consistency and accuracy count.

Practice a rule until it is overlearned. In order for your child to internalize a rule he must practice it to the point that it is overlearned. That means to assure his learning the child must successfully follow the rule on his own many times. The best way to make this happen is to provide a lot of practice with the rule within a short time span. It does not count if your child follows a rule fifteen times without prompting during a three-day period, if interspersed among those occasions there were as many times when he failed to follow the rule or needed a reminder. He has not learned the rule yet.

If the rule you are currently working on involves taking turns while playing a game, your child must have many opportunities to practice sharing activities with different players. Each time he controls his impulses, waiting patiently for his turn, he is reinforcing this habit. The more practice he gets in a short period of time, the better. Invite a friend over to play every afternoon for a week; go to the park playground. One practice session each week for ten weeks is not the same as ten chances to practice in one week or even four or five practice sessions in the course of a weekend. When working on a new rule select a time when you will have at least several opportunities over a few days to practice.

To help you and your child keep track of the rules he masters, copy or use a Rule Card like the one in Figure 12.2. Write the rule you are working on at the top, followed by the rewards and consequences. Every few days rate your child's mastery of that rule according to how often he adheres to it.

When you find that your child is following the rule almost all of the time for a week or longer, then it is ready to be posted on the "Rules I Have Mastered" Chart shown in Figure 12.3. Enter the rule on his chart with great fanfare. Then take a big breath; stick with it, you are ready to teach another rule.

FIGURE 12.2
Rule Card

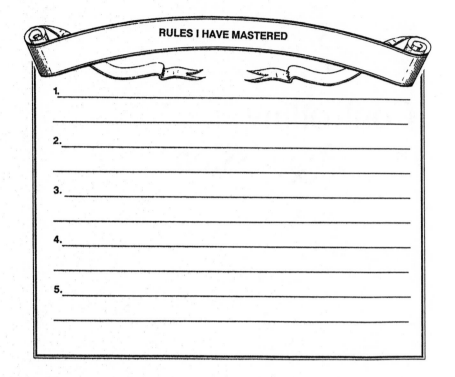

RULES I HAVE MASTERED

1.

2.

3.

4.

5.

FIGURE 12.3
"Rules I Have Mastered" Chart

13

■

Controlling Aggression

*M*ost kids clash occasionally with siblings, peers or parents, and that is normal. They argue, skirmish, maybe cry, and a few sometimes rant and rage. In fact, it would be extremely unusual if a child were never angry or never quarreled with anyone. Some children, though, seem angry and antagonistic most of the time. They react to the smallest things, express indignation, and generally lose their temper with words and fists more than anyone would like. We are always concerned when we see a child with aggressive tendencies, but our worries escalate when the child is also impulsive. Aggressiveness in conjunction with ADHD not only pushes the child into more difficult situations more often but can also signal emotional and behavioral problems that may persist into later life.

None of this is said to panic you. If your child is ADHD and shows signs of aggressiveness, his reactions may also stem from the spiraling frustration he feels as a result of his ongoing experiences at home and school.

Not every child who assumes an offensive stance has long-lasting problems, but your child's aggressive tendencies do warrant your full attention. If the behavior continues or intensifies, you should seek the opinion of a qualified therapist. It is possible that what you are observing is more than simple frustration. On the other hand, by teaching your child a variety of ways to express himself and handle frustration, he may show less hostility, reassuring you that your child's aggressiveness will not remain a problem.

In this chapter we present the attitude you need to adopt and the steps you can take to help your child become less aggressive.

Don't punish aggressiveness with physical punishment. Many parents fall into the trap of fighting fire with fire. Using physical punishment to correct hitting usually does not work. Telling a child not to hit others and then hitting him for doing it really does not make sense. Since children are more likely to model themselves on what they see, "Do as I say not as I do" is rarely effective. In fact, many times we find the root of a child's aggressive behavior lies in the acts he has witnessed or the physical punishment he has received.

Conceivably, a child's aggression might have little or nothing to do with the form of punishment parents employ or the way they handle disagreements between themselves. If your child is frequently the butt of a sibling's or peer's fist, that may contribute to his tendency to physically dominate a younger or smaller child.

Reversing an aggressive trend takes time and supervision. If a child is already combative, you should do everything in your power to remove opportunities for him to model aggression. This may mean structuring interactions with an older sibling or limiting unsupervised playtime with peers who may be able to control their own actions much more easily than the ADHD child. Avoiding aggressive television shows and movies is also strongly advised. Although your youngster may transform any toy into a weapon, you do not have to fill his viewing time and toy chest with guns, spears, pistols and laser weapons. Round out the toy selections with games and building components that promote cooperation and stretch the mind, then spend time playing with those alternatives with your child. Children turn to the pastimes they know best.

Use natural consequences to curtail aggression. Aggressive acts cannot pay off. There is no quicker way to break a pattern. No heart-to-heart talk you can have with your child will promote this point as effectively as natural consequences can.

• Follow aggressive acts with a negative consequence. If an unpleasant consequence follows each time your child hits someone, pushes a friend or destroys an object, he will soon learn he will have to express himself more cautiously. Very routinely, your child should understand that any onslaught, in words or deeds, quickly results in an early ending for playtime. Send a young child immediately to time-out, no warnings necessary. Resume play with the playmate as your child cools his heels in the time-out chair one minute for each year of his age. A neighbor can head for home, as your son heads for his room. If your child hits a sibling in a fight over what TV program to watch, then he should automatically lose his turn and not be able to watch any TV for the rest of the afternoon. These penalties may lead to more immediate anger, but do not worry about that. If you must stand with your hands on your child's shoulders as he struggles in the time-out chair, then do it. He must learn real consequences when he is little. You will not have the benefit of physical dominance on your side when he gets older. Remind yourself that his anger means your limit-setting actions are meaningful to him—they are working.

• Place limits on expressing anger at you. If your child becomes so angry that he begins to vent his hostility toward you, very calmly take steps to limit his reactions. With young children, this means physical restraint. If need be, as you stand behind your child, fold his arms across his chest and hold his wrists in both of your hands until your child starts to relax. No child should ever be allowed to hit you. If he pulls a punch, grip his fist as firmly as possible, instructing him you will let go only when he stops. When he calms down enough to restrain himself, send him to time-out as prescribed.

As children get older and bigger, obviously it's harder to restrain them. If an older child acts aggressively and you sense that any attempt to check him on your part will lead to a wrestling match, then immediately call for a time-out, allowing anyone who needs it a chance to calm down. If he will not walk away, then you should. Use the phrase: "This kind of behavior has a cost. I am going to think about how much as you calm down. I will take into consideration how quickly you are able to calm yourself."

As you think of the possibilities, consider only those consequences you have the control to administer. This approach will help you feel in charge and provide your child with an opportunity, and an often needed excuse, to compose himself.

▪ Use strong consequences that speak for themselves. Another type of logical consequence puts into effect two very powerful techniques called overcorrection and positive practice. Both utilize the logical repercussions of an act as the basis of the consequences. Assume that the child gets mad and throws his plate on the floor. Logically speaking, someone is going to have to clean up the mess. With overcorrection, the child undoes the deed himself—with a little twist. In addition, a larger impression is made by having him not only pick up the pieces of the broken plate and clean up the spilled food but tidy the area around the mess. You have been successful when your child mutters to himself, "It would have been easier not to throw the plate!" In a similar way, if a sibling breaks his sister's toy, it is logical that he should apologize and buy her a replacement with his own money. In addition, to reinforce the action and allow for some overcorrection, he could also do one of her chores for several days to make amends for the unhappiness his careless act caused. The general idea is that he must overcorrect for the damage he has done and practice some positive act that more than makes up for his outburst. Followed to its logical conclusion, overcorrection makes a very effective impression on the child.

Teach the child to use his hesitation and calming response. The best time to intercept an aggressive impulse is before it gains momentum. The hesitation response taught in Chapter 9 and calmness training explained in Chapter 8 can be your child's greatest allies in learning to control aggression. Review both of these coping skills with your child so that he knows how and when to use them. Beyond direct instruction, the best training you can provide is through role-playing. List typical situations where he is likely to lose his temper. A classmate calls him a name, someone cuts in line in front of him or his brother takes his toy. Demonstrate how you would prefer he handle the situation. Talk him through the steps as you act them out. For example, his brother walks into the room with his favorite toy:

- "I hesitate and take one step back from my frightened brother, who realizes he has taken his life in his hands by touching my model X-19 fighter."
- "I think about jumping him, but then I think about him screaming, Mom rushing in to save him and him getting off scot-free while I get punished. I think to myself I am not going to let that happen this time."
- "I begin to use my calming skills to save the day. I breathe slowly, saying 'Relax' as I exhale each breath. My clenched jaw and fists loosen up as I think the word 'relax' to myself."
- "I turn and walk out of the room. My brother is amazed and hurries to put up the toy and hide any evidence of his misdeed, but it is too late. I go to Mom and tell her I am trying to control myself and not kill my brother. She asks what has happened, goes upstairs and catches him desperately trying to stuff all of the parts to the X-19 into the box, and *he* gets into trouble."

Go back and forth alternating roles enough times for him to see how he should behave and to have a chance to practice the new approach in a safe setting so he will be ready when a real opportunity presents itself. Let your child know that you will be watching for any instances when he uses these techniques to control his anger. Praise him each time he tries to use any aspect of this new skill to manage his temper. You may provide extra motivation by implementing some tangible reinforcement, as discussed in Chapter 3, or natural positive consequences, such as extra privileges that relate to the situation. For example, if he controls himself and works out disputes over the television, then extra TV time or an option to rent a video can reinforce his effort. If he plays well with a friend who previously provoked him, then inviting that friend over again or the privilege of having another friend spend the night or go to a movie would be a natural reinforcer.

Teach appropriate assertion of feelings and needs. Often aggressive children do not know how to express appropriately their feelings or assert themselves. They may alternate between passively withdrawing from situations, going off to sulk, and assuming an offensive position, attacking others. Instead of saying, "I am angry at Bill because he chose Jim to be on his team instead of me," the aggressive child is likely to either storm off and miss the game altogether or provoke a fight. When they are having trouble with some job, instead of saying, "I am frustrated," and asking for help, they may throw the book across the room or turn off on the task, refusing to complete the assignment. If this is what you see happening with your child, then use the following techniques to help him learn to assert his feelings and deal with problems better.

• Teach the child to label feelings. It is not always easy to identify your own emotions; imagine how difficult it is for a child. Like any other skill, it takes practice. The simplest way to begin is by talking about feelings in situations that are not personal. As you and your child read a story, ask how he thinks the character is feeling. Look at pictures in magazines and books and probe how he imagines the person is feeling. In all your discussions use very specific descriptions to identify a variety of feelings so that your child naturally expands his vocabulary. Depending on your child's age and, of course, the emotion, use words such as irate, frustrated, irritated, anxious, disappointed, discouraged, furious, dismal, dejected, sad. By adding to his repertoire you are emphasizing the fact that all of us have many different feelings. We can use words to express ourselves. Use the words yourself and prompt your child to use words to communicate what he is feeling.

• Match feelings to situations. Most of us do not express our feelings adequately, we just feel them. However, most of us have learned to control our actions. Your child still needs to learn this. Providing an interim stage in which he identifies his feeling can offer the buffer he needs to ward off impulsive aggressive acts. With your child, identify groups of feeling words and then list all of the situations where in the past he has felt that emotion and which have led to aggressive acts or passive withdrawal. The list developed by eleven-year-old Jonathon and his parents is shown below. Make your list as full as you possibly can. Discuss various experiences that your child has had that may have led to such feelings and then add new ones as he encounters them.

Things that make me mad, angry, irate, infuriated:

_____1. Janie taking my cards. _____

_____2. Billy hitting me. _____

_____3. My sister going into my room and playing with my games. _____

_____4. Mom and Dad not listening to what I have to say. _____

_____5. Having to go to sleep early. _____

_____6. _____

_____7. _____

_____8. _____

Things that frustrate, discourage, dishearten me:

_____1. Trying to work problems. _____

_____2. A very hard puzzle. _____

_____3. Having to redo a messy paper. _____

_____4. Seeing my sister getting good grades. _____

_____5. _____

Things that hurt my feelings, offend me or make me feel resentful:

___**1.** No one asking me to come over. _____

___**2.** Teasing. _____

___**3.** Joey not choosing me for his team first. _____

___**4.** Mom taking Janie's side. _____

___**5.** _____

Things that make me tense and anxious:

___**1.** Being called on in class. _____

___**2.** Having to do a report. _____

___**3.** Going to a party. _____

___**4.** Trying to please dad. _____

___**5.** _____

▪ Encourage your child to label his feelings when he is in a situation. If you see him struggling with a toy that is not working right, say something like, "That looks frustrating." Similarly, if an incident occurs involving your child and a friend, you can validate that it must have "hurt." When he relates a particular occurrence to you, prompt him to use emotion words to express how he felt.

▪ Model appropriate use of feeling words. When you are upset, angry, disappointed, sad, or whatever else, express your feelings out loud so your child will hear you verbalize such experiences in appropriate ways. "I feel so bad that I forgot Aunt Jen's birthday. I hope she won't be hurt or angry with me."

▪ Praise and reward your child every time he uses his feeling words appropriately. Whenever he catches himself and uses words as a way of coping rather than blowing up, let him know exactly what he did right. You might say, "That was very good thinking. You said you were getting tense over the test and asked for help rather than throwing your book." At this point, if you were using a reward system, you would award points or extra privileges because he used an appropriate coping skill.

▪ Review the feeling words list, periodically asking your child to tell you how he is using them to control his temper. Problem-solve with him any situations that are leading to recurring difficulties and generally let him vent his feelings.

▪ When you see him having trouble controlling himself, prompt him to use one of his words. Ask him, "What are you feeling right now?" If this embarrasses him, ask him to help you develop a secret signal, such as pulling your ear or winking, that you can use to remind him without others' knowing about it.

Identify particularly troublesome situations and work on them one at a time. Typically, there are situations that invariably "get our goat." It is like an instant replay every time the situation arises. These negative reactions require extra effort on our part in order to change the pattern. By putting your heads together, you can help your child to use his new skills to "write a new script." Perhaps an ongoing battle in your house ensues over the television set. Bring the siblings together to discuss the problem the family is having. Together you can create a new set of solutions that may work surprisingly well, because everyone has a vested interest. These are the options Jonathon and his brother devised. Some of them are definitely tongue in cheek, but they worked fairly well for this family:

▪ Identify the situation: choosing the television program to watch.
▪ Suggest ways to select television choices and choose option for the week: who gets to the television first (anything under two minutes, move to next option), toss a coin, keep track of turns on tally pad.
▪ Generate a list of phrases that can be used when someone does not agree with the selection: "Dear Brother, I do not like your choice of shows. Could I prevail upon you to try again?"
▪ List positive consequences of coping well: Keep a new world's record of days without a fight over the television. Every five days earns the right to one extra television selection or renting a video.

- Identify negative consequences of an argument about the television: Whoever loses his temper misses television for the rest of the day and loses next selection of following day.

Seek professional help. If your child continues to have chronic problems with aggressiveness or if any of his acts has the potential to cause himself or others harm, then you should seek professional help. Remember such aggressiveness along with ADHD could be symptomatic of more intense underlying emotional or behavioral disorders and is a warning sign that should not be ignored.

14

■

Building Self-Esteem

*I*f there were
but one gift you could give your child, what would it be? You
may find it difficult to select one, but like most parents we meet,
you realize that without a good self-concept or self-esteem the
happiness you wish for your child may elude him. Even the
tycoon who has twenty million dollars in the bank, a loving
wife, three kids, a big house and no mortgage probably senses
some incompleteness unless he feels good about himself. It is
the same reason why a beautiful model with a gorgeous figure
can look in the mirror and find only faults.

While many other children naturally grow up feeling good
about themselves, various research studies have shown that
ADHD children and adults have lower self-esteem and a poor

self-concept. In fact, in some ways this is the most serious outcome of the disorder. Many of the behaviors that get your child into trouble now will pass. Circumstances will change and so will the opportunity for the behavior. How many times does an adult have to wait with hand raised to be called on? When you are the father at the dinner table, you can make an excuse to get up and walk around if you become antsy. Yet long after the situations fade from memory, an individual can be left with negative thoughts and feelings about himself that continue to influence his actions.

By treating each aspect of ADHD as described in this book, you are helping your child with each part of his problem, and indirectly, you are enabling him to build a better self-concept. Still, surviving childhood with a good sense of self requires that self-esteem be built directly.

An accumulation of many experiences, self-concept is never derived in one setting, or for that matter, in one day. Self-concept is the way a child or individual sees himself. He may consider himself a good ball player, a loyal friend, a lousy speller, a fair student and a pretty good joke teller, adding up to numerous concepts of self. His self-esteem, however, is based on how he *feels* about himself. Some of those feelings stem from the discrepancy between his self-concept and the concept of what he thinks he should be. Other feelings are more basic, stemming from the fact that he feels loved because he is a cherished individual. Self-esteem is cumulative, built on the experiences your child amasses through the years. While many of any child's self-images are derived from the value the child places on what he can do, another portion of his sense of self comes from the feelings that he is worthy of love and is loved because *"I am me."* The latter concept demands nothing more of the child than that he be himself. There is a powerful sense of security in knowing that you are loved for no other reason than that you are you.

No one is born with self-esteem. It is learned day by day. Your child's sense of worth began developing when you held him the first time as an infant. Holding him in your arms provided him with a feeling of security. Of course the baby did not say to himself, "This person thinks I am special." Yet over time, when you cuddled him, fed him, responded to the tears or rocked him, that message was learned. Then when he took that first step and you clapped and smiled, he learned something new: "This is something I can do; I am a walker." Daily he added new skills: "I can climb; I can eat with a spoon; I can pour water." Each achievement added a new dimension to his thoughts about himself. Remember your child's glee on these occasions? If we could only keep that wonderful sense of self alive, all our jobs would be very simple.

As a parent, you are one of the most important participants in this process, but certainly not the only one. Others also interact with your child, some casually, others consistently. Every exchange cannot be a compliment, or even positive. Helping any youngster, especially the ADHD child, build and maintain a good self-concept despite the negative comments and interactions is very important.

Some of the methods of increasing self-esteem are built on the same behavioral principles that we use throughout this book. It should not come as a surprise to you that by changing our behavior in positive ways, we build good feelings of self. It is also important, though, to provide a means for a child to monitor what he is saying to himself about himself.

Why do you criticize your child? Probably to help him learn to do something better. When a parent says, "You made a C on that test. If you had studied more, you could have made an A," he intends to be encouraging. Is it fair to say that what you mean is "You are very bright. If you'd give more time to school you could easily make an A?" However, what your child is likely to think is "I am dumb. I didn't do well on another test."

Although we can provide more powerful ways to motivate your child, you are powerless against the criticism that will come his way from others. In this chapter we provide suggestions that will help you contribute to your child's positive sense of self as well as discuss ways you can teach your child to counteract the negative comments of others.

Provide positive feedback to your child about what he is doing right—every step of the way. Make it a regular habit to find something positive to say about what your child is doing.

- Be specific. Avoid global statements and exaggerations. Children know when statements are extreme and they take them for what they're worth. You will be adopting this approach for a long time. Every statement doesn't have to be a jubilation. "This is the prettiest picture I ever saw" may be true but your child is unlikely to believe it. "You used the color yellow so effectively in the flowers in your picture. Looking at this picture makes me feel happy" is likely to be more credible.

- Look for steps toward progress. Sometimes adults appear to value only end products because they neglect to comment on the effort that was required in the process of getting there. For a child, each step along the way is often as important as the goal. Rather than saying, "You're working so slowly, you'll never finish your homework," say, "You have completed three problems correctly; let's see how you do on the next three." That way the message your child hears is "I did three problems right; I can do the next three, too," rather than "I never finish anything." Without a need to be defensive, your child is propelled back into his work.

- Try to maintain a ratio of four positive comments to each negative comment. It is unrealistic to think that you will never say another critical word to your child. After all, perfection is not something we should expect in our children or demand of ourselves. If you can maintain a ratio that permits your child to hear many more true and positive than negative things about himself, not only will you encourage more positive behavior, but also you will both feel better about what you are doing.

- Keep a Good Behavior Diary. Sometimes it is very hard to implement the positive feedback habit. This little book is a tool to build your skills and help everyone feel good about himself.

Record everything your child does right in a small composition book that is easy for you to carry around. At the end of the day or every few days, sit together with your child and review the list.

The Good Behavior Diary can also be used to build specific skills. If you are working on the goal in Chapter 9, impulse control training, then in the diary you can record actions related only to that behavior.

▪ Use "Things I Like About Me" lists. This simple tool not only provides a glimpse into your child's self-concept but also is a helpful conversation opener.

The first time you ask your child to list things he likes about himself, he may find this task difficult. This is true for almost all children. You can offer one statement about yourself to get him started: for example, "I like the way I bake chocolate cake."

▪ Make it a regular part of your interactions. If your child is one who answers each of your queries about what happened at school today with "Nothing," then this technique may elicit more information. Instead of the same old question, next time ask "What's one thing you like about what you did in math today?" In this way you increase communication and help your child accept positive responsibility for his own actions.

▪ Share your list of what you like about your child. Your child knows you love him, but does he know some of the reasons why you like him? He may be quite surprised by your list.

Build a positive inventory of experiences. There are many kinds of self-concept. Think about it as a smorgasbord of thoughts through which your child builds an image of who he is. It includes views of himself at school; his knowledge of a particular subject, of his friends, about sports; his expectations about his intelligence; his sense of humor or his art ability; and almost anything else you might list.

▪ Find activities that your child can feel good about. No one is good at everything, but it is even more important to search for activities through which the ADHD child can find some success. If your child has athletic ability that makes him a natural at team sports, that's great. If not, help him discover other types of sports where he can feel good. Karate or horseback riding, activities in which the child must depend on himself rather than a team, are often successful alternatives. If he does not enjoy sports, look to computers or the arts to enhance his self-esteem.

▪ Set time limits for each activity. A contract can be an effective way to do this. When entering a new pursuit, agree on a reasonable time frame for the trial period and the responsibilities of both parties. Perhaps your son suggests he would like to take piano lessons. Before buying a piano, arrange to rent one or for your son to practice at a neighbor's home for two months. Agree to keep siblings away from the piano for a twenty-minute practice session five days a week. If your child is still excited and practicing as promised, then you will look for a secondhand piano after the trial period.

Counteract the effects of criticism. If praise builds self-esteem, then criticism detracts from it. While criticism is usually intended to be constructive, many children take the words directly to heart—and self-concept. Immediately, the phrase "You didn't make your bed" is translated into "I don't help; I am no good."

• Teach your child a positive way to accept criticism. Help your child counterbalance this tendency by repeating the negative statement (to acknowledge it), making a correcting statement, and then saying to himself that it says nothing about him as a person. In the example, the child would first respond, "You're right, I didn't make my bed, I should do it now," and then say to himself, "I am still a good person."

• Teach your child to respond to unjustified criticism in a nonaggressive way. Sometimes criticism is unjustified. Impulsive children become enmeshed in fights because of their aggressive responses to unfair claims and teasing. Role-play with your child, using a series of obviously erroneous statements, beginning with declarations that cannot possibly be taken seriously. As your child gains the knack of handling these interactions, move to statements that have the ring of truth but are still unjustified. Jeff's mom came up with three statements to use for practice:

"You're a retard . . . You flunk every test."
"What a baby, go drink your bottle."
"You are a spaz, you always drop the ball."

She practiced with Jeff by first demonstrating how to make statements that contradict the claim: "That's silly. I didn't flunk the math exam. I did very well." They played out each situation until Jeff felt confident.

▪ Use role-playing to overcome the effects of negative teasing. Children can be very cruel, teasing each other for any number of reasons—because a child is tall or short, has lost a tooth or has red hair. You can immunize your child against the bad effects of teasing by being prepared. Have your child make a list of the kinds of things children tease him about. It may not be a fun exercise, but the information will help him stand up to goading. Jeff told his mother all the things he could think of that classmates had said during the year. His mom helped him put the phrases in hierarchical order according to which ones hurt him the most.

She asked Jeff not to act hurt but rather to repeat the opposite of the teasing statement silently while staring at the accuser. She then told Jeff to pretend he was one of the guys teasing her. The interchange went like this:

Mom says, "You catch a ball like a two-year-old girl."
Jeff just stares at his mom, but he does look a little hurt.
Mom waits for Jeff to answer. When he doesn't, she says, "Oh,
  forget it! You're no fun to tease!"

Mom told Jeff that was perfect, except next time he should try looking more confident. They went through the same procedures for each statement on Jeff's list.

Identify the negative statements your child is saying to himself. Many times children make negative claims, such as "I'm stupid," "That's something else I can't do right," "I just don't have any brains; I'll never be able to do that." They may also accept certain negative concepts as fact: "I cannot do math," "Tennis will never be my game," "Nobody likes me." Whether it is under the breath or aloud, these beliefs must be identified and replaced by honest more positive ones.

▪ Make a list of the negative statements and their positive counterparts. We all have tapes reverberating in our minds. Ask your child to pretend to play the negative tape that runs when he is feeling bad about himself. List each statement as Jeff did in Figure 14.1. After each negative statement, Jeff's mom helped him create a positive self-statement. They then played a game in which Jeff said the negative statement, pretended to back up the tape in his mind and erase it. He then "recorded" the positive phrase. They practiced the tape recording several times, and Jeff was told to catch the negative tape whenever it started, erase it and record a positive self-statement.

• Set realistic goals and expectations. Self-esteem is measured by the discrepancy between what a child feels he is and what he should be. If a child falls far short of his concept of what he should be, then his self-esteem suffers. If he makes his goal, then his self-esteem is high. However, if the expectations are inappropriate and impossible to achieve, then he cannot possibly feel good.

How does your child feel about himself as a student, a family

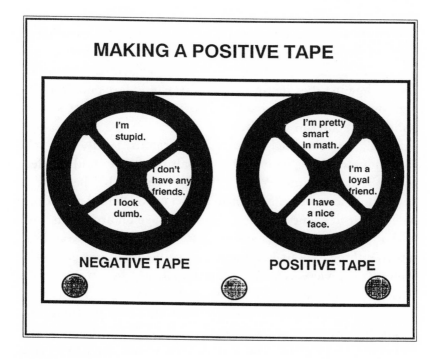

FIGURE 14.1
Negative Self Tapes

member and a friend? How does he feel about his looks? How accurate is your child's estimation of his abilities? How do you view him? It is hard to get children to talk about these things. At the top of a sheet of paper, put the headings *School, Friends, Family* and *Self.* If your child is old enough, ask him to write statements about each area; otherwise, write them for him. Prompt his opinions with questions like: What are your best subjects in school? How would your teacher judge you as a student? What kind of a friend are you? What do your friends like about you? What do you think is your best feature? What do you like about your looks? Next, ask yourself several questions, including: Do you feel there are discrepancies between the way he sees himself and how others view him? How accurate are your child's perceptions of himself? While it is unlikely that you will be able to convince your child that he is wrong, large differences between the way your child feels and how you view him should give you a good idea of areas you need to work on.

Many times a child's expectations of the rest of the world are very unrealistic. From a child's point of view, neighbor Carl may have seven best friends and never gets into trouble. Of course, against that picture, most of us would fare poorly. Helping your child set a realistic goal is an important first step in building a good self-concept.

Again, consider each area: school, friends, family and self. Using a new list, develop realistic goals that your child will feel good about attaining. When Jeff completed his list he decided he would like to be able to make a B on his book report, ask one new friend to spend the night, and not have an argument with his baby sister for three days. He also decided that he would say positive things about his freckles since he could not get rid of them. These were realistic goals that could be attained in a reasonable time period. The grin on Jeff's face when he earned a B+ on his book report and his friend accepted his invitation to spend the night spoke volumes about how he felt about achieving those goals. The fact that he would need to work a little longer on the third and fourth goals did not detract from how he felt.

Academically	Socially	Family	Self
B on book report	Invite a new friend to spend the night.	Not fight with baby sister for three days.	Accept freckles.

- Love your child unconditionally. In the midst of the emotion, sometimes it is hard to show your love for a child who is running you ragged. You know you love your child no matter what, but your child does not have access to that information unless you show it.

15

■

The
ADHD
Child
at Play

*M*any people assume
that if school and behavior problems are managed, then all will
become right in the ADHD child's world. Unfortunately, the
same aspects of ADHD that hurt a child's ability to do his
schoolwork or stay on task also interfere with his social relationships. If a child is impulsive in the classroom, it is a sure
bet he is impetuous on the playground, where there are fewer
limits set to confine his behavior. If his rashness causes him to
interrupt the teacher, who censures his conversation with
friends and family? Even if an ADHD child learns how to hold
his tongue or take turns with a friend, he may not know how to
interact and respond in group gatherings. The ADHD child is
not alert to the social cues that are obvious to his peers. A raised

eyebrow, a pause or a pointed look escapes notice, so he easily misses important signals available to more socially astute on-lookers.

Rampant enthusiasm and reeling attention push the young ADHD child into every aspect of play without a thought of the effects of his actions. Equally troublesome, as the youngster gets older, his impulsiveness may pull him headfirst into whatever suggestions are thrown out by peers so that his decisions are fatefully affected by peer pressure. A socially and emotionally immature ADHD child will benefit from instruction in learning how to get along with others.

From knowing how to greet someone to sustaining friend-ships, ADHD children frequently stand outside the social main-stream, confused by the reactions they get from others. Not listening to a conversation consistently enough to know what is going on certainly makes it hard to join in and keep up with a group. Not keeping his eye on the ball can lead to some embar-rassing moments for the child and frowns from teammates. For the child with a brief attention span, difficulty concentrating frequently makes life difficult, but the child himself may be totally unaware of how his response plays a role in what hap-pens around him.

It is fairly easy to identify when an ADHD child is doing something that gets him into trouble with friends or adults. Nor is it hard to guess why these kids are less likely to be chosen as study partners or teammates. In fact, the younger the child, the more difficult it is for the casual observer to identify the proso-cial skills that make someone well-liked.

The ADHD child is often rated by peers as the least-liked child in their classrooms. What makes one person so likable and another an isolate? What characteristics contribute to popular-ity among peers? What skills improve social relations? Social skills research has begun to focus on these kinds of questions, identifying the positive behaviors that make children and adults admired. Not surprisingly, a person's ability to get along with others is a big part of popularity.

Contrastingly, less appreciated behaviors are the ones most often demonstrated by ADHD boys in particular. In a laboratory classroom, young males are more active, less attentive, noisier and more disruptive. They display more inappropriate and un-expected behaviors and have more frequent negative interac-tions, both verbal and physical, with their peers.

Consider the idea of the socially skilled person for a moment. Do you know someone who always recognizes what to say and how to act in every situation? An individual who is quite able to adapt his behavior to any situation? That person is probably also a genius at avoiding conflict—verbal as well as physical. Smooth is an adjective that comes to mind. Smooth may have too many negative implications, since we wouldn't want to in-timate that a parenting goal is to raise a generation of little con artists. No matter how adroit con men and con women are, they lack respect for the rights and privileges of others, which is certainly a basic social skill.

There are some very good reasons why it is essential for you to work directly to teach your child social skills even when other problems are under control. The socially skilled person is better liked. That in itself provides motivation, but children who are liked receive more positive reinforcement from others so they feel better about themselves. Appropriate social skills also earn other rewards. By learning how to behave well in school, a child absorbs socially acceptable skills that will help him fare well in later life. A student who is able to mind the teacher is more likely to become a good employee. If he is able to interact effectively with customers, he not only earns his salary but also is likely to merit a bonus. More im-portant, if he masters handling irate customers, he'll be able to handle other strangers and more personal relationships with deftness.

Obviously, maintaining positive interactions places demands on the individual. Being a friend or good group member re-quires deference to the needs and desires of others. Before you can teach your child any social skill he must have acquired basic self-control skills, such as those discussed in this book. With these in place, you can begin a gradual process of improv-ing his social skills, but this learning cannot be rushed. It takes more than one day to make a friend, learn to be a good sport, adopt a strategy of thinking first of others, and remember to keep your eye on the ball.

In this chapter we outline a plan for you to use to identify the social skills you want to work on with your child and the strategies you will use to meet those goals. The section entitled Suggested Readings at the end of this book supplies additional resources and materials to assist you. Of course, the best way for a child to learn social skills is in a group setting. There are a growing number of therapists offering social skills training. If you can find such a group nearby, your child will have the opportunity to learn new skills and practice using them in a safe controlled setting.

Pinpoint the social skills that need to be taught. We are social creatures. Each one of us has his strengths and weaknesses when it comes to social situations. One person may love to have people around, relish the thought of a party and never be intimidated by a group of strangers. Another individual in the same family may be more naturally introverted, fear meeting new people and not enjoy spending time in a group. Most of us fall somewhere in the middle, comfortable in some situations, less so in others. Both attitudes are normal. We all feel better when we have a few social skills tucked under our belts. That is how manners got started. By defining socially acceptable means of interacting, individuals learned what was expected of them on various occasions and became more comfortable. Many of these traditions are passed down from one generation to another with much of the instruction provided by time-honored phrases: "Don't chew with your mouth open," "Put your napkin in your lap," "Remember to say please and thank you." Some skills, such as sharing, are considered to be developmental, so parents tend to encourage them, urging an earlier acquisition of the skill. Less often do parents offer instruction on where to stand, how to enter a conversation or accept a compliment. Fortunately many children learn by watching others, so the gaps are less noticeable. Typically, ADHD children exhibit deficits both in their knowledge of social behavior and their performance in social situations. Which skills can you count on your child to display? Which skills are lacking?

The social skills checklist below is an outgrowth of the work and research of Dr. Jimmy L. Middlebrook and Dr. Rena B. Zweben with hundreds of children. Social Skills have been divided into five areas: Basic Skills, Conversational Skills, Interactions with Adults, Interactions with Peers and Expressing Emotions. Copy the checklist and complete it for your child. Consider your child's typical behavior in each social situation; then by circling 1, 2, 3, 4, or 5, indicate how appropriate your child's behavior is under normal circumstances, with 1 meaning not appropriate and 5, very appropriate. Next, circle 1, 2, or 3 to identify how frequently your child does what is being described, with 3 being most frequently. As you move through the list, make notes to yourself about actual situations that you have observed. For example, if your child acts very silly when he is introduced to a new person, jot that observation in the margin. These notes will become valuable as you plan your instructional sequence.

SOCIAL SKILLS CHECKLIST

	How Appropriate?	How Frequent?
Conversational Skills		
1. Introduces self to others.	dk 1 2 3 4 5	1 2 3
2. Introduces two people who don't know one another.	dk 1 2 3 4 5	1 2 3
3. Starts a conversation.	dk 1 2 3 4 5	1 2 3
4. Keeps a conversation going.	dk 1 2 3 4 5	1 2 3
5. Interrupts a conversation.	dk 1 2 3 4 5	1 2 3
6. Ends a conversation.	dk 1 2 3 4 5	1 2 3
7. Gives positive feedback.	dk 1 2 3 4 5	1 2 3
8. Gives critical/negative feedback.	dk 1 2 3 4 5	1 2 3
9. Receives positive feedback.	dk 1 2 3 4 5	1 2 3
10. Receives critical feedback.	dk 1 2 3 4 5	1 2 3
11. Waits turn in conversation.	dk 1 2 3 4 5	1 2 3
12. Demonstrates listening skills in conversation.	dk 1 2 3 4 5	1 2 3
13. Uses telephone for conversation.	dk 1 2 3 4 5	1 2 3
Adult Interactions		
14. Follows directions.	dk 1 2 3 4 5	1 2 3
15. Accepts responsibility for own actions.	dk 1 2 3 4 5	1 2 3
16. Offers help to adults.	dk 1 2 3 4 5	1 2 3

17. Asks for help. dk 1 2 3 4 5   1 2 3
18. Accepts no for an answer. dk 1 2 3 4 5   1 2 3
19. Accepts help from adults. dk 1 2 3 4 5   1 2 3

Peer Interactions
20. Shares. dk 1 2 3 4 5   1 2 3
21. Compromises. dk 1 2 3 4 5   1 2 3
22. Handles being teased. dk 1 2 3 4 5   1 2 3
23. Joins a group. dk 1 2 3 4 5   1 2 3
24. Offers to help. dk 1 2 3 4 5   1 2 3
25. Asserts own opinion. dk 1 2 3 4 5   1 2 3
26. Participates in group activities and games. dk 1 2 3 4 5   1 2 3
27. Handles peer pressure. dk 1 2 3 4 5   1 2 3
28. Handles being left out. dk 1 2 3 4 5   1 2 3
29. Leaves a group. dk 1 2 3 4 5   1 2 3

Handling Emotions
30. Identifies own emotions. dk 1 2 3 4 5   1 2 3
31. Expresses own emotions. dk 1 2 3 4 5   1 2 3
32. Handles other people's anger. dk 1 2 3 4 5   1 2 3
33. Handles own anger. dk 1 2 3 4 5   1 2 3
34. Handles other's failure. dk 1 2 3 4 5   1 2 3
35. Handles own failure. dk 1 2 3 4 5   1 2 3
36. Handles other's success. dk 1 2 3 4 5   1 2 3
37. Handles own success. dk 1 2 3 4 5   1 2 3

Basic Skills
38. Makes eye contact with other person. dk 1 2 3 4 5   1 2 3
39. Keeps pleasant face when conversing. dk 1 2 3 4 5   1 2 3
40. Maintains physical distance between self and others. dk 1 2 3 4 5   1 2 3
41. Speaks in a pleasant voice. dk 1 2 3 4 5   1 2 3
42. Keeps a still and relaxed body. dk 1 2 3 4 5   1 2 3
43. Speaks at an appropriate rate. dk 1 2 3 4 5   1 2 3

dk = don't know

After you complete the checklist, use a highlighter to mark those statements where you indicated your child's behavior was inappropriate most of the time. You can't tackle every skill at once, so prioritize them in terms of the ones that you believe can be taught most directly and select one to work on first. Some skills, such as knowing not to interrupt others, have a great deal to do with your child's impulsiveness. As you work through the chapters of this book, your child will gain the self-control that will make any skill easier to teach.

■ *Understand the Social Skill*

The first step to creating your instructional plan is to consider the particular social skill you have selected in terms of your child's own behavior:

- Where does your child usually have the problem?
- With whom does it usually occur?
- What does your child do in the situation that he shouldn't?
- What does your child not do that he should?
- Do you believe your child knows what to do, or is he unaware of the appropriate way to respond?
- Does your child sometimes exhibit the correct social skill or does he rarely, if ever, respond as he should?

To answer these questions you may need to observe your child's behavior for a few days. The time will be well worth it as you plan your teaching activities. Casually talk with your child about the skill. Robert's father gathered a lot of information by asking his son after they ran into some friends at the mall, "Mr. Akin said hello to you, but you were very quiet. Why?" At first Robert was quite reluctant to answer. When his dad added, "I never quite knew what to say when I met one of your grandmother's friends," Robert felt comfortable admitting, "Yeah, me either."

Define exactly what you need to teach. Most of us underestimate the sophistication required to act competently with aplomb in various social situations. For starters, consider the particular social skill and its components. Greeting someone takes much more than just saying, "Hi!" If you are going to take the time to teach your child the skill, try to be complete. As shown with "greeting someone new," break the skill into all its pieces.

Skill to be taught:
Greeting someone to whom you are introduced.

Components:
Listening to the introduction.
Approaching the person at the correct distance. You can't

yell "Hello," nor do you want to get right in the person's face.

Establish eye contact.

Smile.

Introduce self: "Hello, I'm _____."

Repeat the individual's name in your greeting: "It's very nice to meet you (name)." Or, if you are unsure of the person's name, this is the perfect time to ask for clarification (don't you wish you'd learn to do this, too?).

Provide a little identifying information about yourself that the individual can use to remember you. Examples might be: "I'm Bernice Walker's daughter" or "I go to school with your son Sam."

Pause to allow the person to respond.

If appropriate, ask the person a little bit about herself, but avoid being too personal. Examples: "Is Sam out shopping with you?" or "How is Sam? I haven't seen him."

Repeat that it was very nice to meet the individual and give some form of salutation.

Did you realize how much was involved in that one social interchange? Probably not. Often, though, it is the little pieces of the behavior that are missing that make all the difference. Have you ever spoken to someone who didn't respond to your greeting, left you hanging in the conversation or would not look you straight in the eye? What about the person who wouldn't allow you to return gracefully to what you were doing? To know if your analysis is correct, role-play the skill with your spouse, watch other adults and children and then, try out the skill as you have described it until you feel you have divided the skill into its component parts.

Teach the skill directly. More than discussion, your child will need to try out the skill in a variety of settings, over a long enough period of time for him to feel very comfortable. At that point, he will probably still require practice and perhaps some prompting until the skill becomes second nature.

• Model the skill yourself. With a confederate or by assuming one role after another perform the elements of the skill as your child watches. You will probably need to take all roles as you initiate your instruction. When Robert's father began to teach him how to greet someone, he assumed the roles of introducer, new person, and child. Robert thought this was quite funny but it also got his attention. His father moved from position to position as he took on each role. Actually he had a good time himself.

• Make a checklist for the skill. After modeling, review what you did, asking your child to help you identify the parts of the skill. Robert's father helped him walk through the greeting, replaying parts of the scene to prompt his son's memory. With your child, make a checklist of the necessary components. Although you have already done this, the more information your child is able to contribute, the more meaningful the actions will be to him.

• Have the child model the skill. With the prompts prominently displayed, walk your child through the components of the skill. If he has particular difficulty with any piece of the action, stop to discuss it.

• Play out the scene. Robert and his father reenacted the scene in the mall. Since the memory was still fairly vivid, it provided a natural purpose for the activities. To provide another kind of prompt, Dad first took Robert's role with his son making the introduction. This gave Robert one more opportunity to view an appropriate greeting. Then the pair reversed the roles, with Dad making the introduction and playing the stranger. Robert played himself.

• Offer commentary. The first time you role-play, make it as easy as possible for your child. Give him lots of feedback and be a willing participant, offering encouragement and natural conversation. Always be very specific about what your child does well. After a few giggles, Robert did an excellent job of offering greeting, smiling, looking at his dad and introducing himself. He needed some prompting to remember to offer some information about himself. They reviewed the second part of the scene, replaying it several times before continuing.

• Make role-plays harder. As his son became more comfortable greeting someone, Dad subtly altered the situation. After all, real life is much less predictable than role-plays. In one scenario, he did not immediately respond to the greeting; in another, he responded profusely, so his son was forced to think on his feet. With each situation, his dad told Robert about how well he coped or made suggestions about how he could have handled it another way: "When I did not respond you could have repeated your comment or offered, 'Well, it was very nice to meet you. I'll tell your son I saw you when I see him next time.' " When his son was at a total loss, he prompted him and on the one occasion when he forgot what to do, he let him know that this happens to everyone occasionally.

▪ Ask an ally to help. Before trying it out in a real setting, dad asked mom to role-play an introduction with Robert. This type of situation is as real as you can get but still very safe.

▪ Begin real-world practice. Once your child is comfortable with the role-playing, send him out into the world with a little homework. Ask your child to try his skills in meeting new people at social gatherings and other situations where people are prone to be introducing themselves. Before you attend any event, where it's likely his skills can be put to use, take your child aside and review the skill. Of course you won't have the opportunity to observe all of his actions, but ask him to report on all his attempts—successful or not. More important than the individual performance is your child's reaction. Praise him for all attempts, regardless of the outcome, then ask him which components were the most difficult, how the individual responded and how he felt about the action.

▪ Problem-solve. When things go wrong or when your child encounters situations of which he is unsure, it is important for him to develop some coping skills that will help him through the situation. Just as you taught him the other parts of the skill, role-play these techniques:

Calm myself. Take a deep breath and repeat to myself, "*I can handle this.*" This technique will provide some breathing space for him to identify what he wants to do next. Most children are totally unaware that adults vamp like this.

Define the problem. "What do I want to happen here?" For example, "I can't remember the person's name even though I met him on the bus yesterday."

Generate alternatives for solving the problem.

Say, "Hi!" and fake it until I hear someone mention his name.
Avoid him and pretend I didn't see him.
Reintroduce myself: "Hi, I'm Robert. Please, tell me your name again. It's on the tip of my tongue."

Evaluate the consequences of each alternative. The alternatives could lead to several outcomes:

Looking foolish if someone else comes up who needs to be introduced.
Appear to be a snob.
Risk offending the person because you did not know his name.
None of the above: you might not look foolish and the person might be glad you were interested enough to risk the query.

Select an option. After considering both the positive and negative outcomes, your child will have to select a position and adopt it.

Evaluate the outcome. Give yourself credit for any successes and recognize that you are trying to improve your social skills.

Evaluate what you have learned for the next occasion. Everyone learns from his experiences, and your child can ask himself questions that will help him learn. How did I feel when I said what I did? How do I think the other person felt? Would another alternative have been better?

■ *Dealing with Friendships*

As your child learns one skill after another, his social behavior will become more sophisticated and appropriate. He may naturally begin to make eye contact or be more assertive. As you see, many social skills are not performed in isolation. Your main role is to identify the skills that need to be taught and provide a means for your child to learn them. Helping a youngster become an avid observer as well as a considerate participant in social situations will improve his relationship with others. Still, you will remain a facilitator.

Although you have a large circle of friends and a sibling may be a social butterfly, some children are loners and others have a few close buddies. No parent wants his or her child to be an outsider and every parent feels helpless when he or she feels a child is being excluded. As your child learns his way through the maze of relationships, you have another role to play in helping him find a few good friends. Of course, the younger the child, the more control you have.

MAKING FRIENDS

Plan time with peers. Most children have a very busy activity calendar. Make sure there are opportunities for your child to interact with peers outside of school or organized group activities.

Limit the time and situation. You've probably heard, or said it yourself, "Let them leave while they're still having fun." Until the relationships are well-established, limit the amount of playtime to a couple of hours and plan situations where you can take some control of the action if you must.

Supervise. The age of your child determines the amount of supervision needed and how easily it can be provided. You must structure first-play situations for young children. As youngsters reach the intermediate grades, your presence in the area is helpful, but you cannot directly supervise play. It would embarrass your child. Over time you can move toward less structured, longer playtimes.

Offer coaching. If you are working on a particular skill, such as sharing, talking about it with your child before his playmate arrives prompts the new behavior. Role-play and suggest a game plan that will help your child remember to share. Create a secret sign, like a wink, that will let your child know you noticed his attempts to use his new skills. Although you might gently pull your child aside to offer a suggestion of how to act, avoid criticizing your child in front of his playmate.

BEING REALISTIC ABOUT FRIENDSHIPS

For many children, childhood friendships are transient, changing with the class rolls each year. When your child finds one or two good friends, promote the relationships, but do not be surprised when the connections cool off.

It is easy to attribute every problem with friends to your child's problems. Yet if you talk to other parents and children, you will find many kids have similar difficulties.

■ *Extracurricular Activities*

For many ADHD children, participation in sports is the saving grace of every afternoon. Out on the field, the reflexes take over. For others, the playing field is just one more place to pay attention and concentrate. If your child is a natural athlete who loves sports and performs well, great! By all means, keep him involved in athletics of his choosing! But many ADHD children find it difficult to maintain interest in team sports so that their performance becomes a bone of contention with the other players. Others are not well-coordinated, so that after a while they tire of the uphill struggle. If either scenario sounds familiar, then you may not be achieving your goals. Children like this often enjoy and succeed well in more independently oriented sports activities that have less down time or where the competition is against oneself rather than an opposing team.

Because of the nature of the sport, many team games include a lot of down time for individual players but demand a constant state of readiness. When you are out in left field on the Little League team, you can wait all day for a hit to come your way. However, in one brief second, if your child's eye is not on the ball and your child's mind not on the game, he can blow his chance and the inning and make a number of players unhappy. If your child is going to play a team sport, talk with the coach about a position that keeps him in the thick of the action so it maintains his attention.

We have found that ADHD children, like many other kids, enjoy and succeed at sports where the action is fast-moving or they have more control over their own action. Such sports as tennis, horseback riding and karate, dance or even basketball may fill the bill.

■ *A Final Word*

Do not make the mistake of underestimating how difficult it is for any child to learn how to get along in this world. Most of us would have benefited from a little direct instruction to pave our way. Your child is lucky that you are willing to help ease his path. Social skills are not learned in a day, but your encouragement is an important part of the process.

16

■

The
ADHD
Child
at School

*I*t is no coincidence that it is at school where ADHD first shows up in many children or where it first causes the most problems. Nowhere else is the child required to concentrate so long in the face of so many powerful distracters (commonly called peers). All students must learn class routines, conform to teachers' rules and inhibit their impulses to do otherwise, but adhering to conventions and being organized are terribly difficult for many pupils struggling with ADHD. Complicating their educational experiences more drastically is the fact that up to 75 percent of ADHD youngsters have learning disabilities or at least significant academic skill deficits that make keeping up tough. No wonder so many ADHD youngsters have trouble in school year after year.

Despite the hindrances ADHD causes, do not let the problems your child is having in school overwhelm you. The techniques and skills taught in this book are designed to help your child gain enough self-control to be able to adapt to the requirements of school. He will learn to sit longer, inhibit his desire to blurt out answers, and pay attention to the teacher's directions. Fundamental, however, to his continuing success will be the ability of the school and home to coordinate efforts.

As your child progresses through the educational system, there should be an increasing number of times when his status as a child with an attention deficit disorder will come as a surprise to onlookers or teachers. Until you reach this stage of progress there will probably be occasions when you feel that you are your child's only advocate. Keep in mind that the role you seek is one of facilitator. When you meet with your child's teachers, the primary question for the group must be "How can we work together to promote a successful educational experience for this child?"

It is especially easy when things are not going smoothly to blame the school for some of the problems your child is having. "The teacher's not consistent; he should have been placed in Mrs. _____'s class; this teacher doesn't really have a handle on the whole class." It is not a perfect world, so some of your observations may be correct. On the other hand, do not underestimate the school's desire to help your child. Our experience has shown us time and again how willing teachers are to work with a child and his family to improve an educational experience. But you must be realistic about the limits of the staff's ability and energy to manipulate the environment to serve one student. Your child is only one of many in the classroom. While you should be your child's champion, remember that a team effort involving the school, the child and the parents will reap the greatest return.

For some children, the regular classroom will not be as good a choice as a specialized placement in a smaller, more structured setting where the teacher is especially knowledgeable about teaching strategies for children with ADHD and learning disabilities. For any number of reasons, the child may not meet the criteria for a full-time specialized class placement even though he needs specialized help. Although the student may qualify for resource help several hours a day, that may not be sufficient to overcome his problems. At that point you may want to investigate opportunities for tutorial help after school or a full-time private special-education alternative. However, this is not always feasible or necessary.

No matter what type of classroom or school your child attends or what grade level he is at, you will have to work very closely with the school to help your child overcome problems associated with ADHD. When parents and teachers sit down together with the question "How can we work together for the benefit of this child?" foremost in their minds, there are many steps both inside and outside the classroom that can be taken to help the ADHD child.

You have initiated direct instruction to overcome many of the problems your child is having at home and elsewhere. Almost all the skills you are teaching your child can improve his classroom behavior. However, as we have repeatedly emphasized, the most effective way to overcome the problems associated with ADHD is through direct instruction and interventions that aid that process. In this chapter, we discuss elements related to each of these.

■ *In the Classroom*

Many of the problems that plague the ADHD child during the elementary school years stem from the types of experiences in which he must participate. Recognizing this fact, there are many interventions that can help the ADHD child adjust to life in the classroom.

Type of classroom. While you may have little opportunity to name your child's teacher, the type of classroom in which the child is placed makes a big difference in how easily the child can follow the routines. Invariably, ADHD children perform better in more structured settings headed by teachers who prefer defined work patterns rather than open-ended choices for tasks. Open classrooms, where students accept greater responsibility for their own learning and work schedule, are usually very difficult for this child. A teacher who consistently follows children's behavior with appropriate consequences, both positive and negative, is likely to be the most effective. Classroom routines and definite consequences certainly keep the child headed in the right direction. Most important, the teacher must be willing to make the extra effort that will be needed to keep the ADHD child on task.

Minimize distractions in the classroom. Since many ADHD children are stimulated by their surroundings, it is helpful if the environment is as uncluttered as possible. While many natural distracters exist in any classroom, the ADHD child should not be placed in a seat directly facing the most creative and colorful bulletin boards in the room, the globe, the windows, or worst of all, the communal meeting place of classrooms, the pencil sharpener. Usually placement in the front of the classroom, where most visual distractions will be behind the child, works fairly well, but that position can be a real mistake if the teacher's desk is the spot where all the students come to place their completed papers or get help.

Many ADHD children perform better if they are seated near the source of instruction. Less typically than in the past decades, this is the front of the classroom. Today we most often find teachers are moving targets, rotating from group to group, rarely lecturing from the front of the room. If there is a location that situates the ADHD child away from distractions and yet still in direct line to the teacher, that will be a top choice. The teacher may have to try several locations to find the best one for your child.

Unless it makes him the odd-man-out, the ADHD child should sit at an individual desk rather than at a common table, elbow to elbow with other children. Preferably, he should be situated near peers who are less likely to distract him and more able to withstand the ADHD child's attempts to involve a friend in interesting conversation. Sitting in the midst of role models who are busy getting their work done can be a sobering experience for a child who is looking for others to join him in off-task behavior.

Adjust dosage and scheduling of medication. For those children who need and respond to medication, the dosage and the timing of its administration are very important to the child's ability to concentrate and even to his classroom behavior. As described in Chapter 6, there is no one optimum dosage of medication. By using the feedback system discussed in Chapter 6 as well as the information presented here, with professional supervision, you and the teacher can manipulate the timing of medication to gain the optimum effect during the key periods of the day when attending and self-control are the most important.

Each child's response to a particular medication varies, so both parents and teachers must answer some significant questions:

1. How long does it take for the medicine to begin to have an effect?
   _____ minutes
2. How long does it take until it reaches its peak?
   _____ minutes
3. How long does the effect last?
   _____ minutes/hours

Knowing this, you and the teacher can review your child's daily schedule to determine when he needs to be able to concentrate the most. Use a combined schedule and medication sheet similar to the one depicted for Jess in Figure 16.1.

Jess was having difficulty concentrating during reading instruction. He was a whiz at math and had never experienced any trouble with that subject, but language arts presented a different scenario. An analysis of his schedule indicated that Jess was taking his medication too early in the morning. If the first dose was delayed thirty minutes, it would reach its peak effectiveness during reading group. The effectiveness of the medication during the language-arts block, when Jess had the most written assignments, was a bonus, since it helped improve his handwriting, making his work neater and more legible. He also needed to take the second dose during recess so that he would be able to attend to the afternoon subjects.

Each child's school schedule and response to medication vary, so it is essential to use a similar chart to plan the medi-

Child's Schedule	Medication Effect	
Time	Minimum Effect	Maximum Effect
7:00 Breakfast	(first dose--10 mg)	
8:00 Homeroom-board work	***	
8:30 Math instruction		***
9:00 Math workbook		***
9:30 Language Arts Block		***
10:00 Reading		***
10:30 Spelling		***
11:00 Computer	***	
11:30 Lunch	***	
12:00 Recess	***	
12:30 Social studies	***	
1:30 Science	***	
2:30	(second dose--5 mg.)	
2:30 Art/Music	***	
3:05 Dismissal	***	

FIGURE 16.1

Jess's Daily Schedule

cation schedule. Correcting the timing and dosage of medication can make all the other school interventions work much better.

Break academic tasks into manageable parts. As they become more skilled, all children must learn to work independently for longer periods of time. For the ADHD child this achievement comes harder and usually later than for the typical student. The major sources of interference, as you are well aware, are brief attention span and great distractibility. In Chapters 10 and 11 we introduced the notion of decreasing distractibility and lengthening attention span. As you work through those chapters, you will naturally move toward academic tasks, since generalizing the learning to the classroom is paramount.

In many cases, children with attention deficits are overwhelmed by the amount of work that is expected. In classrooms where teachers distribute several assignments at once so that pupils must operate independently as the teacher instructs small groups, unfinished papers often pile up on the ADHD child's desk. It is not a matter of whether the child understands the tasks. The problem is the length of the exercises and the amount of time he is expected to go it alone. On-task behaviors must be carefully shaped until the child can work independently as long as demanded.

In addition, as with Jess, who adored math, the ability to work independently and maintain attention varied significantly across tasks and subjects. Another child for whom language arts is easy may be able to complete several vocabulary worksheets without looking up, while one page of math problems is impossible for him to complete in one sitting. Half the page or simply two rows might be the most he can accomplish at one time. In that case, this goal would be to increase gradually the number of problems completed in one interval until the child can finish the entire assignment. Even when the child is able to do an intact page in one sitting, he may still find it necessary to cover all but one row of problems or some part of the page to avoid being visually distracted as he works.

As a rule, rather than handing a stack of papers to an ADHD

child, give him only the number of pages or amount of work in the particular subject he can do at one sitting. When he finishes this specific assignment, he may get up to get the next, offering him a natural pause that matches his actual span of attention at that point in development. Of course, where he puts that assignment and picks up the next become crucial factors in his return to work. Each aspect, plus the length of time between work sessions, must be carefully specified or these natural breaks can turn into strolls around the classroom.

Increase attention span for working independently. The team objective must be to gradually increase the ADHD student's attention span for completing assignments. A timer is the key instrument in helping the student shape a longer attention span for work at school. Begin by assisting the student in setting a realistic goal for how long he thinks a particular assignment or set of papers will take him to complete. Write the time goal on the top of the first page. If you know he usually requires ten minutes to complete one workbook sheet and that is a reasonable intermediate objective, then suggesting he can do two pages in the same time frame should be discouraged. Setting small goals that can be easily met is the best approach. Once you have negotiated the time element, the student sets the timer and begins working. If he finishes the assignment before the timer rings, he should note how many minutes remain, calculate the time used and mark the amount next to the original goal. If when the timer rings the task is incomplete, encourage the student to continue to work, noting how much additional time is required so that he can set a more reasonable goal next time. In either case he must execute the assignment legibly and correctly.

The child should be reinforced both for correctly estimating and meeting these endurance goals and for working independently. "You said it would take twelve minutes to do the board work and you did it neatly in eleven."

Over time, the child should be encouraged to increase the length of time he works independently. If he has been completing one row of math problems or one-page assignments, he may now set a time goal for two pages or two tasks, until his behavior more closely matches that of his peers. He should be reinforced for gradually increasing the length of time he can work independently. "You can now work consistently for fifteen minutes doing math problems. That is a new world's record for you." Help him set gradually larger endurance goals and meet them. Remember, fifteen minutes is progress when he used to work for twelve, and sixteen minutes will be even better regardless of whether his classmates presently work for thirty minutes. The key is to have the student compete with himself by setting and beating his own endurance goals.

Reinforce academic behaviors. Setting and meeting attainable endurance goals is reinforcing in and of itself. Praise from the teacher also helps, but most ADHD students require additional reinforcement in the classroom to maintain their motivation. If the teacher already has a reinforcement system operating in the classroom, it can be used to award additional reinforcement for academic behaviors the teacher wants to strengthen. If there is no ongoing reinforcement system already operating in the classroom, then a simple individualized one based on the elements discussed in Chapter 3 and used throughout this book can be employed. Using a system like this, the ADHD student may earn points for each page or assignment correctly completed. Additional bonus points should be conferred for reaching a time goal or breaking an endurance record.

Not all teachers will have a reinforcement system in their classroom or be able to set up an individual one for each ADHD student. A simpler alternative that may work for some teachers and students is to allow the pupil to directly earn additional privileges without using any type of token. There are limitations to the effectiveness of this approach, given the fact that there is usually a delay between work and reward and the ADHD child's inherent problems with delaying gratification, but it is better than no extra reinforcement at all. Extra privileges that could be earned vary from classroom to classroom but might include: time at a favorite activity center in the classroom, extra computer time, a trip to the library, free time at the end of the day to play a game with a friend, or a special job such as line leader.

Decrease ADHD behaviors. In 1975, some colleagues of ours,

Dr. Teodoro Ayllon, D. Layman, and Henry Kandell, found that by rewarding academic performance, hyperactive youngsters not only exhibited more on-task behavior but also displayed fewer inappropriate behaviors, such as getting out of their seat, talking, and other ADHD-related symptoms. Over the years other behavioral psychologists and educators have confirmed their findings. When you consider it, this is such a logical approach. If you reinforce a child for completing increasing amounts of academic work, he will not have as much time to get out of his desk, talk to others, or participate in other off-task behaviors.

Even though reinforcing academics can greatly reduce inappropriate behaviors while the student is working, we all realize that the ADHD youngster can still have behavior problems before, after, and even in the middle of assigned work. Usually additional behavioral strategies will have to be employed to address these problems both in the classroom and elsewhere at school. The best approach is to address each behavioral problem, solving it in a step-by-step fashion. Whenever possible, specify a behavior to reinforce that is the opposite of or is incompatible with the problem. In that way, you can reinforce the positive behavior as well as apply negative consequences to the errant behavior. Although it takes both positive and negative consequences to help the ADHD student learn to follow rules, any program of consequences should be weighted toward positive feedback. Listed below are some typical ADHD behaviors and the incompatible alternatives you would want to reinforce.

ADHD Behavior	Alternative to Be Reinforced
Blurts out questions/comments	Raises hand/waits to be called on
Gets out of desk/wanders	Stays in seat for _____ minutes
Looks around room/doesn't pay attention to directions	Looks at teacher when she talks/ maintains eye contact
Daydreams, doesn't finish work	Works consistently on tasks

Of course there are many other possible examples, and in fact there are times when it may be necessary to actually count the negative as well as the positive behaviors. For example, if you are working on helping a student learn to stay at his desk, it might be feasible to identify a record time to beat (i.e., did not get out of his seat without permission for ＿＿ minutes). Another approach would be to tally the number of times per day the student was out of his seat without permission; then on pursuant days, reinforce him for leaving his seat a fewer number of times (i.e., only got out of his seat without permission four times today versus seven the day before). As progress is made, the count can be extended over days of the week, so that a child is earning points for the number of days in a row he works at his seat as expected. Counts like this are easy to keep track of but have a hidden danger. While they are meaningful tools to the child, you must be careful not to allow lengthy counts of days in a row to take progress for granted. Reinforcement remains an important ingredient in the ADHD child's continuing success. "Reinforce as you go" is a motto to be heeded.

Teach self-monitoring. Most students require supervision, but ADHD youngsters often seem disproportionately to absorb the energy of the teacher. Whenever we start to talk to overburdened teachers about setting up monitoring programs, it seems like an insurmountable responsibility—especially if there is no payoff in behavior change. But if the time requirement is minimal and the results are successful and move in the direction of self-management, teachers are more willing to make the effort. This is again where you can step in and help the teacher. Through the home feedback system described in the next section, you share the responsibility for the classroom program. By monitoring assignment completion and behavior improvements, you have a very good idea of your child's on-task behavior each day.

Since self-control is the ultimate goal, a student should begin to assume responsibility for monitoring his own behavior as soon as possible. In terms of the time goals described above, the ADHD child must be taught to accurately estimate and record his own time goals. Certainly this is less feasible for a first grader, but even a young child can be involved by breaking an assignment into parts, even if he is not yet timing himself: "I think I can do two rows of math problems without stopping or getting up." Likewise, in terms of nonacademic behaviors, a child can learn to record the number of times he gets out of his seat without permission on a card taped to his desk. Of course you should also have him record the positive aspect of the behavior. The card in Figure 16.2 shows how this was done for Neal during certain periods of the day.

Keep the card simple. Add one period at a time, usually starting from the early A.M. The child may not be able to accurately keep track of time, so it is sometimes more helpful to describe the time periods in terms of activities. Using scheduled time frames allows the teacher to check the student's accuracy on a regular schedule. At the start, the teacher must check the card frequently, initialing when she agrees with the child's record. The child should earn an extra point for reliable recording. However, if the child's record and the teacher's observations for the period disagree, then he should earn neither a point for

	Neal's **IN SEAT CARD**		
Time of Day	**# of Times Out of Seat**		**+ = Stayed in Seat Whole Period**
1. 8:30-9:00 Language Arts	*//*		
2. 9:00-10:00 Reading	*/*		
3.. 10:00-10:45 Math			**+**
4. 10:45-11:15 Music			**+**
5. 11:15-11:45 Lunch			
6. 11:45-12:15 Recess			
7. 12:15-1:00 Creative Writing	*//*		
8. 1:00-1:45 Social Studies			**+**
9. 1:45-2:30 Science			**+**

FIGURE 16.2

Neal's In Seat Record

improved behavior nor a point for accurate recording. At the same time the child should be told not to worry; he has another opportunity to earn points during the next recording period. Without any reference to lying, the teacher should specify her observations: "Neal, remember, you got out of your desk and went to the pencil sharpener without permission." As the child progresses, more periods can be added.

When the point is reached that more than six periods are being recorded, rather than adding additional periods, lengthen the individual time frames, so board work and reading are collapsed into one period with double points awarded. Very gradually, as the child gains control over this one behavior, many children reach the point where they have a card that is divided into two segments, A.M. and P.M. After a number of weeks of this, the child may be able to switch to a count of days in a row with no unauthorized out-of-seat behavior.

■ *Between Home and School*

What makes the most difference to any child's commitment to succeed in school is parental support and expectations. Your role is probably most significant in that respect. Yet unlike other parents who may rely on the school to involve them when help is needed, you must offer your direct support from the very beginning. Although you cannot and should not be in the classroom each day, your child will know that you are involved and interested if a home feedback system is in place.

Design a school/home feedback system. School-to-home feedback systems can take many forms. The key, as always, is simplicity. A teacher must be able to keep track of the system every day of the year, not just when everything is going smoothly. This means that the system must be designed so the child is motivated to help keep the record and get it home.

If your teacher has a classroom reinforcement system already in place, then she may simply send your child's record or a copy home at the end of the day. Of course if a copy is to be made, your child will probably have to do the copying. If this is the case, he should be given a stack of forms to use. With that done, the teacher only has to check the accuracy of the child's copy and sign off. The most obvious way to motivate your child to reproduce the record and bring it home is to award extra points for doing so.

Depending on the form of the record, it could summarize either how well your child worked in school or how well he behaved, or both. By allowing your child to trade in his school points at home, you make these points doubly valuable, so he is encouraged to earn more at school the next day. In Chapter 3 we discussed ideas for a menu from which your child might choose ways to spend his points at home.

If your child's teacher does not have her own reinforcement system, or if you need to focus on specific behaviors that are not covered in hers, there are a number of simple alternatives.

▪ Use a self-monitoring card. Like the one used for Neal in Figure 16.2, this card can easily be used to record and monitor one behavior. Because it is immediately portable, it's a simple matter to bring it home each day.

▪ Measure activity level and work completed. An alternative is a report card like the one shown on page 85. The advantage of this card is that it will work for a great number of teaching styles and classrooms. From first grade to high school, many teachers have adapted this feedback system to the needs of an individual child. The stack of books represents a gross measure of how well the child completed the tasks assigned to him during the day. The right side, as shown, offers a gross measure of activity level. In Figure 16.3 the card has been adapted so that the meter on the right measures the amount of time the child remains in his seat when he is expected to do so. Cards like these can be used period by period during the day, morning and afternoon or for the entire day.

As always, any monitoring and reinforcement system should begin with a time frame for which the child can be successful. One child might receive a card for each task; for other children, another division, like subject matter, might be more appropriate. In a few weeks, you can enlarge the time frame so fewer cards are needed while the same level of academic activity is encouraged.

Reinforce the child for participating in the system. This is crucial and often overlooked. Your child is a conduit between home and school. All children, but ADHD kids especially, are notorious for not remembering books, coats and assignments, much less reinforcement cards. When you initiate the system, begin by rewarding your child for bringing home the card regardless of what it says.

▪ Use activities to reward him for bringing home his card. In a sense, the card should become the child's ticket to all after-school activities. As long as he filled it in and had it validated by the teacher he should be able to participate in his basic activities. The better his performance, the more special privileges he earns. We have found this formula goes a long way toward motivating a child to remember to have his card filled in and brought home. If he knows he will not get in trouble no matter how bad the card looks, he will get it home through rain, sleet and pressuring peers. When these rules are followed consistently, we have observed ADHD students who could not re-

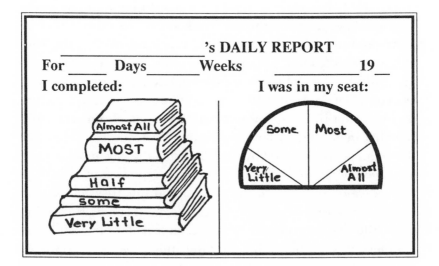

FIGURE 16.3
Report Card

member their coats in a blizzard pleading with a teacher to validate their cards at the end of the day.

 • Gradually reward your child for increasing performance at school. Once your child is consistently bringing home the card, additional points should be awarded for maintaining and improving his record. He may earn one point for bringing home the card, one point for maintaining his behavior or two for improving it. These points can be accumulated and exchanged for items on a menu of your design.

DEALING WITH HOMEWORK

Even when you get school under control, homework frequently remains an issue over which the parents and children continually bump heads. Within this book, we have provided specific techniques to lengthen attention span and reduce distractibility that will help with homework also. Other factors will come into play in a successful homework plan.

 • Bringing home assignments and getting them back to school. There is no great payoff for doing your homework but not getting it to school. Leaving books, assignments and papers at school or home is a constant source of frustration for teachers, children and parents. In any homework strategy this has to be step one.

The easiest approach is to tie the assignment to the reinforcement system. Literally, have the child staple the assignment to his feedback card. In the beginning, regardless of how much work is completed, he should also earn extra points or privileges for bringing home his assignments and materials.

 • One work spot. There should be one designated spot for school materials. Most children work most efficiently at a desk. A well-lit corner of the child's room with sufficient work surface is ideal, but if possible, this should be his study spot and no one else's.

 • Timing of homework. Does your child need a break after school or is it better to begin the endeavor immediately, using breaks to reinforce the effort? You know your child best. For ADHD children, medication may have been timed to peak during the school day. When your child arrives home, the effects of the medication are waning so that your child could use some time to play before gearing up to concentrate. Other parents worry that medication given later in the day will interfere with the child's sleep pattern. There are ways to manipulate the dosage so that most of these concerns can be remedied. If after working out a homework plan you find your child is still unable to concentrate, it may be wise to arrange the medication schedule so that your child is able to work at home more easily. If you prefer not to administer medication, perhaps you should allow your child some free time to play and you some time to complete your own chores before gearing up to concentrate on homework.

• Review the homework assignment with your child, breaking each task into manageable units. Although there are likely to be natural breaks between assignments, help your child divide subject assignments into smaller parts. Eventually your child may be able to assume this responsibility or work subject by subject. As before, have your child set time goals for each exercise, using the timer to manipulate the effort.

• Supervise the homework effort. The younger the child and the more severe the problems, the greater the need for supervision. Initially you must be available to oversee homework. As your child completes one part of the assignment, you will reinforce his effort for calculating his time and working consistently. Then repeat the process, helping him determine the next work unit, estimating the time required and initiating work. As your child becomes more successful at meeting his time goals for each part of the task, begin to wean him from direct observation. Initiate the task as usual, then step away from the area, returning frequently to say, "Good work," or pat him on the back. When the timer rings, return to reinforce him and observe the calculation and setting of the next goal. Over time you should be able to remove yourself from more of the task by having your child start the second assignment or work for long time frames before you check his progress.

As we began this chapter, we said school is often the first place where ADHD shows up. For many years, school will remain a concern, but you will feel better about it as you work with your child and his teachers so that he gains the most benefit from his educational environment. It is an ongoing process, but one where you can very definitely see a payoff in your child's attitude, his academic performance and the reactions of his peers and teachers. Eventually your child's school career will come to a conclusion. Although one's education is never over, eventually your son or daughter will no longer have to sit in a classroom unless he so chooses. Given the skills he has learned, he will be able to set his pace and follow his own interests. He will be ready to head into what is fondly referred to as the real world.

17

■

The ADHD Child Grown Up

*A*ll parents worry about their children, but when your child has a problem like ADHD, concerns easily multiply. Will he outgrow his hyperactivity or will it continue throughout his life? If he finds it difficult to finish his schoolwork now, how will he manage a college load? Will his impulsiveness and resistance to authority interfere with his ability to hold down a good job?

As we work with parents, there's an adage we like to share. We call it the hundred-foot rule and it goes something like this: Do not worry about anything more than a hundred feet or a hundred days ahead of you. If you take care of your child's todays, then most of the tomorrows will take care of themselves.

We believe that. If you, as a parent of an ADHD child, can also accept that notion and know that by adopting the approach offered in this book you are working on today, you will feel more comfortable about the future. Few goals worth accomplishing are attained overnight. No parent's job is an easy one, but yours requires more management than most. The aspirations you have for your child are worth accomplishing, but they will not be achieved instantaneously. Do not let these words discourage you; take heart from the fact that you have time to help your child gain the self-control he needs. If you take it one day at a time, skill by skill, both you and your child will reach your goals.

ADHD children do grow up. On some days that time probably seems very far away indeed, but we all know that it happens sooner than we expect. Professionals once thought that when ADHD youngsters reached puberty, their problems would be over. They would outgrow many of the characteristics of the attention deficit hyperactivity disorder. We know now that this is only partially true. Perhaps one-third to one-half of ADHD children outgrow the overactive aspects of their behavior but remain distractible. Many of these children continue to have problems with restlessness, concentration, short attention span and impulsiveness.

In the last twenty years ADHD has become the most researched topic of all the childhood behavior disorders. Much of the research has focused on the efficacy of medication and the role of interventions in educating the ADHD child. There have been retrospective studies of the childhoods of individuals diagnosed as ADHD as adults, as well as prospective studies that followed ADHD children as they grew into adulthood. These latter studies, like the body of longitudinal research conducted between 1960 and 1975 at Montreal Children's Hospital and McGill University, are very important because both the retrospective studies, which provide hindsight, and the prospective studies, which carry a future orientation, tell us what happens to the ADHD child when he grows up. What factors predict what you and I might consider a good or poor outcome? In addition, such studies can provide valuable insights into what the ADHD adult thinks and feels about the syndrome that characterizes so much of his history.

ADHD children do grow up. In fact, as adults, many of them are indistinguishable from their peers. Just as in any population of adults, some have more problems adapting to the responsibility of adulthood. Perhaps they no longer have troubles in the classroom, but some individuals change jobs or move more frequently than might be expected. To alleviate some of your fears, studies of hyperactive adults indicate that they were gainfully employed and economically self-sufficient, ably maintaining steady jobs, although sometimes their economic status was not as great as they might like. For this and other reasons, as you might imagine, some of the ADHD adults among the groups studied frequently did not have high self-esteem or a good self-concept.

The problem with drug involvement, which is rampant among young adults in general, also shows up among ADHD youths, but not necessarily to a greater degree. Some ADHD adults do have more problems with antisocial behavior. This is especially true if as a child and adolescent, the child exhibited additional conduct disorder symptoms that complicated the diagnosis. One factor, the presence of very aggressive tendencies that are not ameliorated over the years by therapy, definitely places the ADHD child at risk. You must remember that most of the time the collection of characteristics collectively labeled ADHD do not appear in isolation. Seventy-five percent of these individuals have additional learning disabilities that play a significant role in the child's ease of learning, as well as in his ultimate educational attainment.

All the news is not bad. Negative outcomes are neither final nor written in stone. That is why we wrote this book. ADHD children whose problems are diagnosed early and who are the recipients of combined interventions over a period of years are more successful. ADHD children of greater intelligence who are reared in stable families appear to have an advantage, but all children can fare better with consistent help. Most important is the fact that ADHD children whose therapy assumes a long-term view that is directed toward individual symptoms of the disorder have more positive outcomes.

There is much we can learn from the insights of ADHD adults. Repeatedly they point to a significant individual in their lives—a parent, teacher, therapist or friend—who helped them, listened to them and talked with them. They also note how helpful it would have been if someone—doctor, parent or psychologist or teacher—had explained the various aspects of their problems. This is clearly shown in relation to the use of medication. Regardless of the benefits of any pharmaceutical intervention, the negative feelings these children experienced toward pills might have been lessened if they had more clearly understood the role of medication in controlling various aspects of the disorder. As it was, they resented medication because it made them feel different or ashamed when other children discovered it. If they had understood that they had problems that were no fault of their own, like diabetes, then many of them may not have accepted the notion that they were dumb or bad. Like the diabetic who must control his intake of sugar, they would have understood and accepted the responsibility for working toward control of the aspects of their behavior that can be troubling. These adults did not understand ADHD. Their parents cannot be faulted because they did not understand either. Your child is luckier. You do understand.

Not too long ago we received a letter from an adult who had read in the *Atlanta Journal and Constitution* one of our columns, which happened to be about ADHD. He asked us to give the parents and youngsters we work with a very special message. He said, "Tell them, 'Don't give up! It can all turn out okay!' " He told of the relief at finding out what his problem was and of the successful treatment that he had put together for himself over the years. As he put it "I may not have been destined to be an air-traffic controller," but as a businessman in sales he had been very successful and was happy. As long as he had a good secretary to keep him organized, he could put his energy to use in the most productive way. He added that these days when his co-workers call him "hyper," they say it with envy, as his sales totals for the month accumulate.

This man's story epitomizes many of the things you and your family must keep in mind over the years. Once a diagnosis was made, this man educated himself about ADHD. Then knowing himself better, he searched for and found the treatment programs that addressed the problems with which he had to deal. This is an important point.

The core symptoms of ADHD that characterize your child's behavior now are likely to remain, but the symptoms will not manifest themselves in the same ways as your child grows up. First of all, as you work your way through the chapters of this book you will be dealing directly with each of the symptoms that affect your child so that he learns to control his behavior.

As his attention span grows, many other behaviors will be less apparent. He will be less distractible and more able to concentrate. Yet when your child hits the adolescent years and a new school where he must matriculate across classes and from teacher to teacher, he may require additional help to head off potential problems. There are quite a lot of new distracters and competing stimuli in the middle school and high school settings. You and your family must anticipate and plan ahead.

Adolescence is a difficult time for most teens. A constant period of uncertainty, emotional highs and lows, fill the weeks. In a classic sense, most teens feel an increasing need to assert their independence while they strive to stay in step with their peers. This is a time when youngsters who do not grasp the role of medication and therapy, and even those who do, may rebel against taking prescribed drugs or any therapeutic intervention. Yet this is just the time when your son or daughter may need the support of other kids like themselves. Led by a professional, a teen support group with others like themselves who are struggling with ADHD or other problems might be very helpful. Adolescents have many questions about how to behave —around the opposite sex especially. ADHD children find social interactions particularly incomprehensible. While an ADHD youngster may resent therapy, he could be responsive to an instructional group centered on social skills.

You may be asking, At what point do I get to sit back? Will it ever let up? That is like asking if parents ever stop worrying or trying to help their children.

As we told you at the start of this book, our experience indicates that the most successful families are the ones who take a long-term view of ADHD. It is something everyone will learn to cope with over the years. There will be periods of time when everything goes fairly well. Perhaps your child has been in individual therapy for a while. You have also been working on a particular problem, like distractibility or impulsiveness, and have achieved some success, so everyone takes a break and lets the new skills and a little maturity take over. Then you will hit a few pebbles. Do not overlook them. Define the problem and design a new plan. If you need additional help, return to work with the professionals you have come to trust, until you come to a point you can glide along on some new mastery.

Your child will grow up. Because you have worked together all along, he will be ready to assume responsibility and make decisions for himself; he will know how to cope.

■ *Appendix A*

The materials and charts used in this book may be copied for your personal use or may be purchased. For a catalog of materials, please send a stamped self-addressed envelope to:

Parents' ED
c/o The Behavioral Institute of Atlanta
5555 Peachtree Dunwoody Road
Suite 106
Atlanta, Georgia 30342

Drs. Marianne and Stephen Garber and Robyn Freedman Spizman are available as speakers, workshop leaders and consultants. For more information, please contact us at:

The Behavioral Institute of Atlanta
5555 Peachtree Dunwoody Road
Suite 106
Atlanta, Georgia 30342
404-256-9325

■ *Appendix B*

FINDING/STARTING A SUPPORT GROUP

All support groups share a common goal—that of helping the members deal with a problem they have. Through continuing education, but especially by sharing information and successes, members learn new ways to cope with the problems that concern them. As a parent or teacher of a child with ADHD characteristics, there is much you have to gain and a lot you have to offer to other parents like yourself. With the support of trained professionals, such groups often form bonds that strengthen everyone in the group.

The information for contacting both the Learning Disabilities Association (LDA) and Children with Attention Deficit Disorders (CHADD) is listed below. If you are interested in starting a support group in your area these points will help you.

• Contact one or more professionals with a strong interest and background in ADHD who would be willing to assist you. Professionals who may be interested in joining the effort include psychologists, psychiatrists, pediatricians, family practitioners, neurologists and teachers.

• Form a steering committee of both parents and professionals to guide the formation and development of the support group. This committee can appoint acting officers to conduct business for the young chapter.

• Select a time, location and topic for your first session. Locate an easily accessible space that can accommodate at least fifty people.

• Use the network of neighborhood and parenting newspapers, local radio stations, school newsletters and flyers to announce the formation of the support group.

▪ Gather information about nationwide organizations so you can determine if you want to affiliate with one of them. We are familiar with two nationwide organizations you should know about. The Learning Disabilities Association (LDA), formerly the Association for Children and Adults with Learning Disabilities, is a nonprofit organization that has 50 state affiliates with more than 800 local chapters. The total membership is over 60,000 parents and professional persons. This organization is dedicated to defining and finding solutions for the broad spectrum of learning disabilities.

Children with Attention Deficit Disorders (CHADD) is a nonprofit organization that was started in Plantation, Florida, by local professionals and parents of children diagnosed ADHD. Now there are over 165 chapters nationwide and a newsletter the organization sends to its membership.

The addresses for these two organizations are listed below.

Learning Disabilities Association
4156 Library Road
Pittsburgh, Pennsylvania 15234

Children with Attention Deficit Disorders
499 Northwest 70th Avenue
Suite 308
Plantation, Florida 33171
(305) 587-3700

■ Suggested Readings

ATTENTION DEFICIT DISORDER AND HYPERACTIVITY

Books marked with an asterisk (*) were written for a professional audience.

Barkley, Russell. *Hyperactive Children: A Handbook for Diagnosis and Treatment.* New York: Guilford Press, 1981.*

Bittenger, Marvin L. *Living with Our Hyperactive Children: Parents' Own Stories.* New York: BPS Books, Inc., 1977.

Conners, Keith, and Wells, Karen C. *Hyperkinetic Children: A Neuropsychosocial Approach.* Beverly Hills: Sage Publications, 1986.*

Ingersoll, Barbara. *Your Hyperactive Child, A Parent's Guide to Coping with Attention Deficit Disorder.* New York: Doubleday, 1988.

Kendall, Philip, and Braswell, Lauren. *Cognitive-Behavioral Therapy for Impulsive Children.* New York: Guilford Press, 1985.*

Kirby, Edward A., and Grimley, Liam K. *Understanding and Treating Attention Deficit Disorder.* New York: Pergamon Press, 1986.

Lahey, Benjamin. *Behavior Therapy with Hyperactive and Learning Disabled Children.* New York: Oxford University Press, 1979.*

Lavin, Paul. *Parenting the Overactive Child: Alternatives to Drug Therapy.* Lanham, Md.: Madison Books, 1989.

McWhirter, Jeffries. *The Learning Disabled Child: A School and Family Concern.* Champaign, Ill.: Research Press, 1977.

O'Leary, K. Daniel. *Mommy, I Can't Sit Still: Coping with the Hyperactive and Hyperaggressive Child.* New York: New Horizon Press, 1984.

Parker, Harvey C. *The ADD Hyperactivity Workbook for Parents, Teachers, and Kids.* Plantation, Fla.: Impact Publications, 1988.

Safer, Daniel J., and Allen, Richard P. *Hyperactive Children: Diagnosis and Management.* Baltimore: University Park Press, 1976.*

Silver, Larry. *The Misunderstood Child: A Guide for Parents of Learning Disabled Children.* New York: McGraw-Hill Book Co., 1984.

Taylor, John F. *The Hyperactive Child and the Family: The Complete What-to-Do Handbook.* Everest House, 1980.

Weiss, Gabrielle, and Hechtman, Lily Trokenberg. *Hyperactive Children Grown Up.* New York: Guilford Press, 1986.*

Wender, Paul H. *The Hyperactive Child, Adolescent, and Adult: Attention Deficit Disorder Through the Lifespan.* New York: Oxford University Press, 1987.

SOCIAL SKILLS

Cartledge, Gwendolyn, and Milburn, Joanne Fellows, eds. *Teaching Social Skills to Children.* New York: Pergamon Press, 1986.

Clabby, John F., and Elias, Maurice J. *Teach Your Child Decision Making.* New York: Doubleday, 1987.

Gurian, Anita, and Fomanek, Ruth. *The Socially Competent Child.* Boston: Houghton Mifflin Company, 1983.

Osman, Betty B., with Blinder, Henriette. *No One to Play With.* New York: Warner Books, 1982.

Scott, Sharon. *Peer Pressure Reversal.* Amherst, Mass.: Human Resource Development Press, 1985.

GENERAL PARENTING

Bateman, Lawrence, with Riche, Robert. *The Nine Most Troublesome Teenage Problems and How to Solve Them.* New York: Ballantine Books, 1986.

Becker, Wesley C. *Parents Are Teachers.* Champaign, Ill.: Research Press, 1971.

Caplan, Frank, general editor. *The Parenting Advisor* by the Princeton Center for Infancy, New York: Doubleday, 1978.

Clark, Lynn, *SOS! Help for Parents*. Bowling Green, Ky.: Parents Press, 1985.

Forehand, Rex L., and McMahon, Robert J. *Helping the Noncompliant Child: A Clinician's Guide to Parent Training*. New York: Guilford Press, 1981.*

Garber, Stephen W.; Garber, Marianne Daniels; and Spizman, Robyn Freedman. *Good Behavior*. New York: Villard Books, 1987.

Ilg, Frances; Ames, Louis Bates; and Baker, Sidney M. *Child Behavior: Specific Advice on Problems of Child Behavior*. New York: Harper & Row, 1981.

Patterson, Gerald R. *Living with Children*. Champaign, Ill.: Research Press, 1976.

Schaefer, Charles E., and Millman, Howard L. *How to Help Children with Common Problems*. New York: New American Library, 1981.

Spizman, Robyn Freedman. *Lollipop Grapes & Clothespin Critters: Quick, on-the-Spot Remedies for Restless Children 2–10*. Reading, Mass.: Addison-Wesley, 1985.

SELF-ESTEEM

Briggs, Dorothy Corkvill. *Your Child's Self Esteem*. New York: Dolphin Books, 1975.

Phillips, Debora. *How to Give Your Child a Great Self-Image*. New York: Random House, 1989.

RELAXATION

Benson, Herbert. *The Relaxation Response*. New York: William Morrow, 1975.

Jacobson, Edmund. *You Must Relax*. New York: McGraw-Hill, 1934.

Rosen, Gerald. *The Relaxation Book: An Illustrated Self-Help Program*. Englewood Cliffs, N.J.: Prentice-Hall, 1977.

Stroebel, Charles F. "The Quieting Response." *Manual and Audio Cassette Program*. New York: BMA Publications, 1978.

Stroebel, Elizabeth; Stroebel, Charles F.; and Holland, Margaret. "Kiddie QR." *Manual and Audio Cassette Program*. Wethersfield, Conn.: QR Institute, 1980.

■ References

Achenbach, T. and Edlebrock, C. *Child Behavior Checklist (CBCL)*. Burlington: Department of Psychiatry, University of Vermont, 1983.

Anastopoulos, A. D., and Barkley, Russell A. "Biological Factors in Attention Deficit-Hyperactivity Disorder." *The Behavior Therapist* 11, 3 (1988): 47–53.

Ayllon, T. A.; Layman, D.; and Kandell, H. J. "A Behavioral-Educational Alternative to Control of Hyperactive Children." *Journal of Applied Behavioral Analysis* 8 (1975): 137–46.

Barkley, Russell A. *Hyperactive Children: A Handbook for Diagnosis and Treatment*. New York: Guilford Press, 1981.

Barkley, R. A. "President's Message." *Clinical Child Psychology Newsletter* 3, 2 (Fall 1988): 1–2, Division 12, American Psychological Association.

Barkley, R., and Cunningham, C., in *Treatment of Hyperactive and Learning Disordered Children*, edited by R. Knight and D. Bakker. Baltimore: University Park Press, 1980.

Benson, Herbert. *The Relaxation Response*. New York: William Morrow, 1975.

Conners, C. K. *Conners' Rating Scales*. North Tonawanda, N.Y.: Multihealth Systems, Inc., 1984.

Conners, C. K. "A Teacher Rating Scale for Use in Drug Studies with Children." *American Journal of Psychiatry* 126 (1969): 884.

Deutsch, K. "Genetic Factors in Attention Deficit Disorders." Paper presented at Symposium on Disorders of the Brain and Development and Cognition, 1987, Boston, Massachusetts.

Diagnostic and Statistical Manual of Mental Disorders. I(1952), II(1968), III(1974), III-R(1987). Washington, D.C.: American Psychiatric Association.

Douglas, V. I. "Stop, Look, and Listen: The Problem of Sustained Attention and Impulse Control in Hyperactive and Normal Children." *Canadian Journal of Behavioral Science* 4 (1972): 159–82.

Feingold, B. F. *Why Your Child Is Hyperactive.* New York: Random House, 1975.

Gerber, Adele. "Historical Trends in the Field of Learning Disabilities: An Overview." In *Language and Learning Disabilities,* edited by Adele Gerber and Diane N. Bryen. Baltimore: University Park Press, 1981.

Gordon, Michael. *Gordon Diagnostic Systems.* New York: De-Witt.

Hall, R. Vance, and Hall, Marilyn C. *How to Use Time Out.* Austin: Pro-Ed, 1980.

Jacobson, Edmund. *You Must Relax.* New York: McGraw-Hill, 1934.

Kirby, E., and Grimley, L. *Understanding and Treating Attention Deficit Disorder.* New York: Pergamon, 1986.

Lahey, Benjamin B. *Behavior Therapy with Hyperactive and Learning Disabled Children.* New York: Oxford University Press, 1979.

Meichenbaum, D., and Goodman, J. "Training Impulsive Children to Talk to Themselves: A Means of Developing Self Control." *Journal of Abnormal Psychology* 77 (1971): 115–26.

O'Leary, Daniel. *Mommy, I Can't Sit Still.* New York: New Horizon Press, 1984.

Rosen, Gerald M. *The Relaxation Book: An Illustrated Self-Help Program.* Englewood Cliffs, N.J.: Prentice-Hall, 1977.

Routh, D. K.; Schroeder, C. S.; and O'Tuama, L. "Development of Activity Level in Children." *Developmental Psychology* 10 (1974): 163–68.

Rutter, M. L. "Brain Damage Syndromes in Childhood: Concepts and Findings." *Journal of Child Psychology and Psychiatry* 139 (1977): 21–33.

Safer, D. J. "A Familial Factor in Minimal Brain Dysfunction." *Behavior Genetics* 3 (1973): 175–86.

Safer, D. J., and Allen, R. P. *Hyperactive Children: Diagnosis and Management*. Baltimore: University Press, 1976.

Spitzer, R., ed. *Diagnostic and Statistical Manual of Mental Disorders*. Washington, D.C.: American Psychiatric Association Press, 1980.

Sprague, R., and Troupe, L. "Relationship Between Activity Level and Delay of Reinforcement in the Retarded." *Journal of Experimental Child Psychology* 3 (1966): 390–97.

Stroebel, Charles F. "The Quieting Response." *Manual and Audio Cassette Program*. New York: BMA Publications, 1978.

Ullman, Rina K.; Sleator, Esther K.; and Sprague, Robert L. *ADD-H Comprehensive Teacher's Rating Scale*. Champaign, Ill.: Metritech, n.d.

Weiss, Gabrielle, and Hechtman, Lily. *Hyperactive Children Grown Up*. New York: Guilford Press, 1986.

▪ *Index*

Achenbach, T. M., 29
ACTeRs, *see* ADD-H Comprehensive
    Teacher's Rating Scale
activity level, 89–107
    and beat the clock game, 97–104
    and difficulty in following rules, 154
    and endurance training, 104–107
    and statue game, 91–97
ADD, *see* attention deficit disorder
ADD-H Comprehensive Teacher's
    Rating Scale (ACTeRs), 29
ADHD, *see* attention deficit
    hyperactivity disorder
adolescents:
    and drug abuse, 218
    and explaining ADHD to, 61–63
    and medication, 79
    and support groups for, 220
adults, ADHD, 217–20
aggression, 164–73
    and appropriate assertion of feelings
      and needs, 169–72
    and hesitation response for, 168–69
    and identifying troublesome
      situations, 172–73
    and natural consequences for, 166–
      68
    and punishment for, 165–66
    and relaxation training for, 168–69
    and seeking professional help for, 173
alcohol, 14
Allen (case study), 153
allergies, 23–24
American Psychiatric Association
    (APA), 8
Anastopoulos, Arthur, 13
APA, *see* American Psychiatric
    Association
appetite suppression, 76–77
arm exercises, 112
Association for Children and Adults
    with Learning Disabilities, *see*
    Learning Disabilities Association
Atlanta Journal and Constitution, 219
attention deficit disorder (ADD), 8
attention deficit disorder with or
    without hyperactivity, 8–9
attention deficit hyperactivity disorder
    (ADHD), 6, 9–10
    and causes of (theories), 10–16
    diagnosing, 17–34

and explaining to child, 52–63
and gaining acceptance and support
    from family, 64–70
and gaining acceptance and support
    from others who interact with
    child, 71
and gaining acceptance and support
    from teachers, 70
and suggested readings concerning,
    225–26
symptoms of, 9
attention span, 140–51
    and demonstrating paying attention,
      141–44
    and hints for paying attention (illus.),
      143
    and "I can pay attention card"
      (illus.), 146
    increasing for working independently
      in school, 205–206
    and letting child practice on own,
      150–51
    and selecting new target behavior,
      151
    summary chart (illus.), 149
    tape, 144
    tape (illus.), 145, 147
    and teaching child to measure his,
      144–48
    and working on specific tasks, 148–
      50
Ayllon, Teodoro, 207
Azrin, Nathan, 50

Barkley, Russell, 11, 13, 27, 78
beat the clock game, 97–104
    clockcards (illus.), 100, 103
behavior:
    academic, reinforcing, 206
    attention checklist, 33
    changing, 36
    and changing with negative
      consequences, 48–51
    and changing with positive
      principles, 36–40
    and daily monitoring of, 84–88
    diary, 39
    and motivating positive, 35–51
    and periodic monitoring of, 83–84
    and praising positive, 39
    and reinforcement for positive, 40–48

behavior (*cont.*)
  and your record of verbal statements
    concerning (illus.), 38
  see also behavior problems
behavior problems:
  activity level, 89–107
  in adults, 218
  aggression, 164–73
  and anticipating the consequences of,
    154
  attention span, 140–51
  and changes in terminology for, 5–10
  decreasing, 206–208
  distractions, 127–39
  following rules, 152–63
  impulsiveness, 117–26
  social, 184–97
  types of, 5–10
  see also individual types
The Behavioral Institute of Atlanta, 222
birth history, 12–13
body of longitudinal research, 217–18
brain as control center (illus.), 60
brain damage, minimal (MBD), 6–7
brain dysfunction, 13
brain dysfunction, minimal (MBD), 7
breathing, diaphragm, 111–12

Cal (case study), 3–4, 53–54, 56–57
calmness training, *see* relaxation
    training
Carl (case study), 118, 119, 122, 123
CBCL, *see* Child Behavior Checklist
CHADD, *see* Children with Attention
    Deficit Disorders
charts:
  progress, 44–45
  sources for, 222
Child Behavior Checklist (CBCL), 29
Children with Attention Deficit
    Disorders (CHADD), 224
Chris (case study), 131–32, 137–39
clockcards (illus.), 100, 103
  with endurance goals (illus.), 106
Conners, C. Keith, 27
Conners Parent Rating Scale (CPRS),
    27
Conners Teacher Rating Scale, (CTRS),
    28–29
CPRS, *see* Conners Parent Rating Scale
CTRS, *see* Conners Teacher Rating
    Scale
Cunningham, Charles, 11
Cylert, *see* pemoline

d-amphetamines (Dexedrine), 81
  Dexedrine Spansule, 81
Dexedrine, *see* d-amphetamines
Diagnostic and Statistical Manual, 8
Diagnostic and Statistical Manual-II, 8
Diagnostic and Statistical Manual-III, 8
*Diagnostic and Statistical Manual-III-
    Revised*, 9, 10
diagnostic process, 18–34
  checklist, 32–33
  early warning checklist, 21

and early warning signs of ADHD,
    18–21
  medical exams, 22–25
  parent questionnaires, 25–28
  psychological evaluations, 29–30
  and pulling it all together, 31
  teacher ratings, 28–29
diary, good behavior, 39
  for building self-esteem, 177–78
diet, 13–14
Dilantin, 14
discipline, definition of, 36
distractions, 127–39
  and distract-o-meter, 129
  and distract-o-meter (illus.), 131
  list of (illus.), 130
  and making a list of, 128–29
  and personal progress card, 137
  and personal progress card (illus.), 138
  and recording accomplishments
    concerning, 135
  zapper log, 135
  zapper log (illus.), 136
  and zapping during academic tasks,
    135–39
  and zapping during play, 133–34
  and zapping during simple tasks,
    134–35
  and zapping techniques for, 129–33
Douglas, Virginia, 8
drug abuse, 79, 218
drugs, *see* medication

education, *see* school
endurance training, 104–107
  and clockcard with endurance goals
    (illus.), 106
environment, 13–14
Evan (case study), 3, 18–19
exercises, *see* relaxation training
extracurricular activities, 196–97

family support, 66–70
Feingold, Benjamin, 14, 23
friendships, 194–96

games:
  beat the clock, 97–104
  for relaxation training, 110–13
  statue, 91–97
Gilles de la Tourette's syndrome, *see*
    Tourette's syndrome
Good Behavior, xv, 40
grandparents, 68–69
Greg (case study), 127–28, 129
growth patterns, 77

hearing problems, 22–23
heredity, 12
hesitation response:
  for controlling aggression, 168–69
Home Situation Questionnaire (HSQ),
    27–28
homework, dealing with, 213–14
HSQ, *see* Home Situation
    Questionnaire

human variation, normal, 14–16
hundred-foot rule, 216–17
hyperactivity, 7–8
hyperthyroidism, *see* thyroid disease
hypothyroidism, *see* thyroid disease

imipramine (Tofranil), 82
impulsiveness, 117–26
  acts and consequences (illus.), 120
  and difficulty in following rules, 153–
    54
  and explaining concept of, 118–19
  and giving recognition for mastery
    of, 126
  and "I am impulsive" list (illus.), 121
  and "I can control myself" list
    (illus.), 125
  and "I'm in control" cards (illus.),
    122, 123
  and mass practicing for controlling,
    123–24
  and positive practice and
    overcorrection for, 124–25
  and prioritizing the situation, 120
  and reinforcing nonimpulsive
    responses, 124
  and specifying controlled response
    for, 123
  and teaching a hesitation response
    for, 120–23
  versus planned acts (illus.), 119
inattentiveness:
  and following rules, 152–53
insomnia, 77–78

Jacobson, Edmund, 109
Jake (case study), 109
Jamie (case study), 54–56
Jeff (case study), 179–81
Jerilyn (case study), 148
Jess (case study), 202–203, 204
Jessie (case study), 3
Jim (case study), 41, 44–45
Jonathan (case study), 53, 57–58
Jonathon (case study), 170–71, 172–73

Kandell, Henry, 207

Layman, D., 207
LDA, *see* Learning Disabilities
    Association
lead, 14
Learning Disabilities Association
    (LDA), 224
leg exercises, 113
The Little Engine Who Could (Watty), 57

Mal (case study), 129
Mark (case study), 156
materials, sources for, 222
MBD, *see* brain damage, minimal;
    brain dysfunction, minimal
McGill University, 217
medical exams, 22–25
  checklist, 32
  for medication monitoring, 83

medication, 72–88
  and ADHD adults having understood
    about, 219
  and adjusting for school, 202–204
  anticonvulsant, 14
  and daily report card for monitoring,
    84, 85–86
  and daily report card for monitoring
    (illus.), 85
  d-amphetamines (Dexedrine), 81
  and dependency on, 79
  fast-acting, 81
  and how they work, 75–76
  imipramine (Tofranil), 82
  methylphenidate (Ritalin), 72, 74, 76,
    81
  and monitoring system for, 83–88
  and optimum dosage of, 82
  and outgrowing need for, 79–80
  pemoline (Cylert), 76, 82
  side effects, 76–79
  slow-release, 81
  and summary report chart for
    monitoring, 86
  and summary report chart for
    monitoring (illus.), 87
  and the right one, 81–82
  and when to take, 80–81
  without proper testing first, 75
  and your child's response to, 74–75
methylphenidate (Ritalin), 72, 74, 76,
    81
Ritalin SR, 81
Middlebrook, Jimmy L., 188
Montreal Children's Hospital, 217

negative consequences, 48–51
  and overcorrection, 50–51
  and time-out, 49–50
negative self tapes (illus.), 181
nervous tics, 78
  see also Tourette's syndrome
neurological problems, 24–25
nicotine, 14
normal curve (illus.), 15

overcorrection, 50–51
  for controlling aggression, 167–68
  for following rules, 158
  for impulsiveness, 24–25
overlearning:
  to help in following rules, 161

parenting, general:
  and suggested readings concerning,
    226–27
parents:
  and interactions with children, 11–
    12
  questionnaires, 25–28
  record of verbal statements (illus.),
    38
  see also family support
Parents ED, 222
paying attention, *see* attention span
pemoline (Cylert), 76, 82

petit mal seizure, 24–25
phenobarbital, 14
playing, *see* social skills
point system, 40–48
    banks (illus.), 42, 43, 95
    for following rules, 159
    as reinforcement for school, 213
positive practice:
    for following rules, 158
    for impulsiveness, 124–25
progressive relaxation techniques, *see*
    relaxation training
psychological evaluations, 29–30
    checklist, 32–33
puberty, 217
    see also adolescents

questionnaires, parent, 25–28
    Conners Parent Rating Scale, 27
    Home Situation Questionnaire, 27–
    28
    Werry-Weiss-Peters Activity Rating
    Scale, 26–27
questionnaires, teacher:
    ADD-H Comprehensive Teacher's
    Rating Scale, 29
    Child Behavior Checklist, 29
    Conners Teacher Rating Scale, 28–29

reinforcement, effective, 40–48
    activities, as reward, 212–13
    for participation in system at school,
    212–13
    point system, 40–48, 213
    progress chart, 44–45
    progress chart (illus.), 45
    survey (illus.), 47
    see also point system
relaxation training, 108–16
    arm exercises, 112
    contract (illus.), 116
    for controlling aggression, 168–69
    diaphragm breathing, 111–12
    leg exercises, 113
    scoreboard (illus.), 114
    and suggested readings concerning,
    227–28
    yawning game, 110–11
report cards, 84, 85–86, 211
    illustrated, 85, 212
rewards, *see* point system;
    reinforcement, effective
Ritalin, *see* methylphenidate
Robert (case study), 190, 192–93
Roger (case study), 66, 67
Ronnie (case study), 90–91
rules, 152–63
    and adding one at a time, 155
    and being specific about, 155
    card (illus.), 162
    and multiple prompts for, 155–56
    and positive and negative natural
    consequences for, 157–59
    and practicing until overlearned, 161
    and providing immediate feedback
    about, 156–57

and reasons for difficulty in
    following, 152–54
and reinforcement for, 159–61
and response cost for, 159–61
and reward system for, 159
and "rules I've mastered" chart
    (illus.), 163
and setting new records, 159
success chart (illus.), 160

school, 198–215
    and adjusting medication for, 202–
    204
    and dealing with homework, 213–
    14
    and decreasing ADHD behaviors in,
    206–208
    and designing a school/home
    feedback system, 210–11
    and educational evaluation checklist,
    33
    and gaining acceptance and support
    from teachers, 70
    and increasing attention span in,
    205–206
    and learning to work independently
    in, 204–205
    and minimizing distractions in
    classroom, 201–202
    and parental support, 210–11
    and reinforcing academic behaviors
    in, 206
    and reinforcing child, 212–13
    schedule, daily (illus.), 203
    and self-monitoring card for, 211
    and self-monitoring card for (illus.),
    209
    and self-monitoring report card for,
    84, 85–86, 211
    and self-monitoring report card for
    (illus.), 85, 212
    and specialized class placement,
    199–200
    and teacher ratings, 28–29
    and teaching self-monitoring for,
    208–10
    and type of classroom, 200–201
self-control, *see* impulsiveness
self-esteem, 174–83
    and building a positive inventory of
    experiences, 178–79
    and counteracting the effects of
    criticism, 179–81
    and how your child feels about
    himself, 181–83
    and keeping a good behavior diary,
    177–78
    and making a list of negative
    statements, 180–81
    and negative self tapes (illus.), 181
    and providing positive feedback,
    177
    and setting realistic goals and
    expectations, 181–83
    and suggested readings concerning,
    227

and "things I like about me" lists, 178
and unconditional love, 183
Seth (case study), 97–98
siblings, 66–68
side effects, medication:
   appetite suppression, 76–77
   emotional, 78
   insomnia, 77–78
   nervous tics, 78
   physical, 78
sitting still, *see* activity level
social skills, 184–97
   adult interactions, 188–89
   basic, 189
   checklist, 188–89
   conversational, 188
   and dealing with friendships, 194–96
   and defining what you need to teach, 190–91
   and extracurricular activities, 196–97
   handling emotions, 189
   peer interactions, 189
   and pinpointing the ones needing to be taught, 187–89
   and suggested readings concerning, 226

and teaching skill directly, 191–94
statue game, 91–97
   and staircase to success charts (illus.), 92, 94
support, gaining, 64–71
support groups, 220, 223–24

teachers:
   and gaining acceptance and support from, 70
   questionnaires, 28–29
thyroid disease, 22
time-out, 49–50
Tofranil, *see* imipramine
Tourette's syndrome, 78
toxins, 14

Walt (case study), 105, 106
Werry-Weiss-Peters Activity Rating Scale (W.W.P.A.R.S.), 26–27
W.W.P.A.R.S., *see* Werry-Weiss-Peters Activity Rating Scale

yawning game, 110–11

zapper log, 135
   illustrated, 136
Zweben, Rena B., 188

■ *About the Authors*

Stephen W. Garber, Ph.D., is a practicing behavioral psychologist in private practice. He is the director of the Behavioral Institute of Atlanta and a consultant to hospitals, schools and child-care facilities.

Dr. Garber works with children, adolescents and adults with various learning, emotional and behavior problems and advises parents, teachers, pediatricians and other specialists. His special interest in children who are hyperactive and who have attentional problems led to the authorship of this book. Along with his wife, Marianne, he also appears regularly as a member of the Parenting Team on NBC affiliate WXIA-TV's *Noonday.*

Marianne Daniels Garber, Ph.D., is an educational consultant on the staff of the Behavioral Institute in Atlanta. An active speaker on parenting issues and a former teacher at elementary, undergraduate and graduate levels, Dr. Garber also advises parents, teachers and other specialists about learning and behavior problems children experience. Dr. Garber conducts workshops for parents, schools and other professionals about discipline and attention deficit hyperactivity disorder. The Garbers live in Atlanta, Georgia, with their three children.

Robyn Freedman Spizman has published twenty-eight books and numerous articles for parents and teachers on art education and crafts and on enhancing children's learning. She appears weekly as a consumer expert on kids' issues on *Noonday* for NBC affiliate WXIA-TV in Atlanta. She holds a Bachelor of Visual Arts in Arts Education and has taught art in a variety of settings from elementary school to adult education. She lectures exten-

sively and conducts workshops on teaching parents how to cre-
atively motivate their children. She is married, has two
children and lives in Atlanta.

Marianne and Stephen Garber and **Robyn Freedman Spizman**
are the authors of the successful parenting book *Good Behavior*.
They also write the weekly newspaper column "Good Behavior"
and have created a line of greeting cards for children.